P9-CDE-754

Worcester v. Georgia:
american indian rights

SUPREME COURT MILESTONES

Worcester v. Georgia:

American Indian Rights

SUSAN DUDLEY GOLD

Marshall Cavendish
Benchmark
New York

Marshall Cavendish Benchmark
99 White Plains Rd.
Tarrytown, NY 10591-5502
www.marshallcavendish.us

Library of Congress Cataloging-in-Publication Data

Gold, Susan Dudley.
    Worcester v. Georgia : American Indian rights / by Susan Dudley Gold.
        p. cm. — (Supreme Court Milestones)
    Includes bibliographical references and index.
    ISBN 978-0-7614-2956-2
    1. Worcester, S. A. (Samuel Austin), 1798-1859—Trials, litigation, etc.—History.
2. Cherokee Indians—Georgia—Legal status, laws, etc.—History. 3. Cherokee Indians—
Trials, litigation, etc.—History. 4. Indians of North America— Georgia—Legal status,
laws, etc.—History. 5. Indians of North America—Georgia—Civil rights—History.
6. Georgia—Trials, litigation, etc.—History. I. Title.
    KF228.C4594G65 2008
    342.7308'72—dc22

2007050437

Photo research by Connie Gardner

Cover photo by Bettmann/CORBIS

The photographs in this book are used by permission and through the courtesy of:
Corbis: Bettmann, 1–2, 3; Archivo Iconografico, S.A., 61; *AP Photo*: 110; Gerald Herbert,
114; *Alamy*: North Wind Picture Archive, 6, 70; *The Image Works*: Print Collection, 81; *Art
Resource*: National Portrait Gallery, Smithsonian Institution, 17, 94; Smithsonian
American Art Museum, Washington DC, 29; *Getty Images*: Hulton Archive, 26–27, 84,
86; *The Granger Collection*: 52, 67, 76.

Publisher: Michelle Bisson
Art Director: Anahid Hamparian
Series Designer: Sonia Chaghatzbanian

Printed in Malaysia
1 3 5 6 4 2

contents

A COPY OF A MEDAL ENGLISH OFFICIALS PRESENTED TO AMERICAN INDIAN CHIEFS AND LEADING WARRIORS IN 1764 TO PROMOTE PEACE BETWEEN THE TRIBES AND THE COLONISTS.

introduction
A National Treasure

In 1832 President Andrew Jackson defied a U.S. Supreme Court ruling and ordered the removal of more than 16,000 members of the Cherokee Nation from their homes in Georgia. An estimated one-quarter of the tribe died along the trail during their enforced march to Oklahoma. The route they followed became known as the Trail of Tears.

The Supreme Court had no army at its disposal to enforce its ruling—only the law and the U.S. Constitution. Jackson, who did have an army to carry out his orders, disregarded both. Not only did Jackson's order cause immeasurable suffering to the Cherokee, it also violated the very basis of the American democratic system. Jackson's decision to rule by force rather than by law tipped the U.S. Constitution's carefully laid out balance of power between the courts and the executive branch. "That is the system that protects our constitutional liberties," said U.S. Supreme Court Justice Stephen Breyer. Jackson's actions, Breyer said, led to "a dangerous episode in the Court's history, and a tragic story in the history of the Cherokee tribe." John Marshall, the chief justice who presided over the Court in Jackson's time, had doubts about whether the Court or the Constitution would remain intact.

Fortunately, though, the story behind the court case,

Worcester v. *Georgia*, is also a tale of indomitable spirit. The Cherokee have survived; so have the Constitution and the U.S. Supreme Court.

Today the Cherokee tribe is recognized as a separate nation within the United States, with its own government, court system, and laws. The largest two branches of the tribe are based in Oklahoma. Members of a third branch, the Eastern Band of the Cherokee Indians, live in North Carolina. They are descendants of those who escaped into the hills during Jackson's removal efforts. The tribes have built a thriving community within territory held in trust for the Cherokee by the U.S. government. They still practice their ancient rituals; storytellers recite the oral histories of the Cherokee to the next generation. Despite the hardships of past centuries, the people and their culture endure.

After Jackson's arbitrary decision to override the Supreme Court, other officials also attempted to ignore the high court's rulings. When the Court ordered schools in the South to desegregate in the 1950s, most southern governors initially resisted but ultimately complied. "When the Supreme Court speaks, that's the law," Governor Jim Folsom of Alabama said after the 1954 ruling in *Brown* v. *Board of Education* banned school segregation.

Even so, some continued to challenge the Court's ruling. In 1956 nineteen senators and seventy-seven House members signed the "Southern Manifesto." The document charged that the Supreme Court's decision was "a clear abuse of judicial power" and that the ruling created an "explosive and dangerous condition." The signers pledged to "use all lawful means" to reverse the decision; the manifesto, however, helped spur a massive resistance movement, whose leaders often resorted to illegal actions. The Ku Klux Klan, lynch mobs, and violent protesters terrorized southern blacks and their supporters. Although local law officers in certain areas ignored the violence—and in some cases actively participated in it—neither the federal government nor the president endorsed efforts to defy the Court, as in the case of Andrew Jackson and the Cherokee removal.

In 1957 Orval E. Faubus, governor of Arkansas, ordered the state National Guard to block black students from entering Little Rock's Central High School. But unlike Jackson, who sided with Georgia against the Supreme Court, President Dwight D. Eisenhower ordered the 101st Airborne Division to enforce desegregation at the school.

In more recent times, controversial Supreme Court rulings that infuriated much of the population have inspired criticism but not official defiance. Decisions that granted women the right to abortions, barred prayer in the schools, and named George W. Bush as the winner of the 2000 presidential election were "very hard issues," according to Justice Breyer. "But I haven't seen any paratroopers. I didn't see in any of those cases a need for the state militia, the federal militia. There were not bullets; there were not guns in the streets."

In the more than a century and a half since Jackson defied the Supreme Court, the nation has come to realize the importance of the court system in safeguarding America's laws. "This fundamental trust in the law, this habit of following the law, this respect for the rule of law, helps to bind together our three hundred million people as a Nation," Justice Breyer observed. "Not all peoples in all nations resolve their disputes according to the rule of law. We do. And that is a national treasure."

CONSTITUTION

OF THE

CHEROKEE NATION,

MADE AND ESTABLISHED

AT A

GENERAL CONVENTION OF DELEGATES,

DULY AUTHORISED FOR THAT PURPOSE.

AT

NEW ECHOTA,

JULY 26, 1827.

The Cherokee Nation adopted its own constitution, based on the U.S. Constitution, in 1827.

one
A CIVILIZED NATION

Econnaunuxulgee, THE CHEROKEE word for Americans, means "people-greedily-grasping-after-land." The Cherokee tribe originally occupied a large tract of land in what is now the southeastern United States. Their first encounters with English traders in the 1600s were generally peaceful. An outbreak of smallpox among slaves who were brought to the region swept through Indian villages in the late 1600s. The Indians had never been exposed to smallpox and had no resistance to the disease. In some villages smallpox killed the entire population. Almost half the Cherokee population in the Southeast died from the disease.

By the early 1700s the tribe had come under pressure from another threat: the growing number of colonists in their territory. In 1715 the Cherokee banded with other tribes and threatened to demolish the South Carolina colony. The British colonists eventually made peace with the tribes, giving them firearms and other gifts to ease relations.

As time went on, the colonists cut back on the gifts offered to the Indians. Dishonest traders took advantage of the Indians and further increased tensions. By 1754 when the French and Indian War broke out in North America, the earlier bond between the Cherokee and the English was in tatters. Angered by Cherokee trade with the French, the governor of the South Carolina colony sent 1,300 troops into Cherokee territory to stop the tribe from doing business with the enemy. The Cherokee rejected the governor's demands and instead attacked the British garrison. After a number of skirmishes that left many colonists and Indians dead, leaders of the two forces negotiated a cease-fire.

During the American Revolution, the Cherokee, like most other tribes, sided with the British. Their forays along the frontier in Georgia, North Carolina, South Carolina, and Virginia sparked intense hatred among the American rebels. In retaliation, the Americans adopted a "scorched earth" policy, destroying Indian villages throughout the region. The tribe later sought peace with the American revolutionaries.

Americans' voracious appetite for land led to constant friction between the tribe and the white settlers infringing on their territory. President Thomas Jefferson's solution to the problem was to move the tribe west. Shortly before he left office, Jefferson wrote to the Cherokee pledging federal support for tribe members who migrated west, "where game is abundant." The government, Jefferson wrote, would exchange the land they left in the East for the new property in the West. Referring to the tribe's leaders as "my children," Jefferson offered additional enticements to those who agreed to the exchange.

> Every aid towards their removal, and what will be necessary for them there, will then be freely administered to them, and, when established in their new settlements, we shall still consider them as our children, give them the benefit of exchanging their [pelts] for what they will want at our factories, and always hold them firmly by the hand.

Although clearly encouraging the move, the president assured those who stayed in the East that they would continue to receive "our patronage, our aid, and good neighborhood." A few Cherokee took Jefferson's advice and migrated west. Complications arose, however, when the Cherokee who remained behind refused to cede any portion of the land they occupied.

separate and "civilized"

In the Treaty of Hopewell, signed on November 28, 1785, the United States recognized the Cherokee tribe as a separate nation with the power to make peace, declare war, own land, and govern its people. After the American Revolution several southern tribes developed prosperous farms on their tribal lands. Five of the tribes—Creek, Cherokee, Chickasaw, Choctaw, and Seminole—became known as the Five Civilized Tribes because of their adoption of American ways of life, including conversion to Christianity. The Cherokee, in particular, embraced much of American culture. In the early 1800s the tribe turned from its traditional clan system and set up a system of government patterned after the new American democracy. They established their capital in New Echota in northern Georgia in 1825, elected John Ross as principal chief, voted for delegates to represent them in the nation's legislature, opened schools supported by taxes, and organized a court system. A supreme court provided for appeals of lower court decisions. The Cherokee Nation's legislature had two houses, similar to that of the U.S. Congress except that the members of the lower house elected those serving in the upper house. In 1827 the Cherokee adopted a constitution modeled on the U.S. document. That same year the tribe incorporated to become the Cherokee Nation.

The tribe also had its own written language, developed by Sequoyah (also known as George Gist), the son of a

JOHN ROSS: CHEROKEE CHIEF WHO "WALKED TALL AND CAST A LONG SHADOW"

Chief John Ross of the Cherokee led his people in the bitter fight to keep their ancestral lands in the East and continued at the helm after the tribe was forced to move to Indian Territory in the West. A decade or more before Congress mandated the move and the U.S. Supreme Court handed down the *Worcester* decision, Ross spearheaded the Cherokee establishment of a democratic system of government modeled on that of the United States. He became the Cherokee Nation's first president (or principal chief) of the National Council. The Cherokee people elected him ten times to the leadership post—a term that stretched to an astounding thirty-eight years. He served as the tribe's top elected official until his death in 1866.

Ross's father, Daniel, came from a line of prominent Scottish traders who had settled in Georgia before the Revolutionary War. Daniel Ross established a store among the Cherokee in the South and married a woman of Cherokee and Scottish heritage. Born in 1790, Ross grew up among the Cherokee tribe in the Georgia-Tennessee region. A private tutor taught Ross and his brother at home, and Ross received further instruction at a Tennessee academy. Ross's Cherokee name as a boy was Tasman-Usda or Tsan Usdi (Little John). He spoke both English and Cherokee. Later, as an adult, he would be given the Indian name of Kooweskoowe. As a young man he earned the respect of white officials after accomplishing a successful mission to the Cherokee tribe in Arkansas.

During the War of 1812 he fought with other tribal

members in the Cherokee regiment. Under General Andrew Jackson's command, he fought with Davy Crockett, Sam Houston, and Indian soldiers to defeat the Creek, allies of the British. By the end of the war he had attained the rank of lieutenant.

In 1817 Ross moved to Georgia to serve as a member of the Cherokee Nation's tribal council. By then Georgia and the U.S. government had begun efforts to move the tribe from the state to unsettled lands in the West. The tribe elected Ross as its head in 1819, a position he held until 1826. Working with the tribal council's powerful John Ridge and other leaders, Ross guided the Cherokee as they formed a new type of government based on the American democratic system. After helping draft the nation's constitution in 1827, he became the tribe's first president under the new system.

A handsome man with dark hair and penetrating eyes that looked out from under bushy eyebrows, Ross acted and dressed like a country gentleman. At ease in both Indian and white societies, Ross was a cultured man who wore a stylish top hat, top coat, vest, and trousers to his meetings with the rich and powerful in Washington, D.C., and elsewhere. He was one of the wealthiest merchants in northern Georgia in the 1830s and also owned a two-hundred-acre plantation and numerous slaves.

Despite all his contacts in Washington and his determination to preserve his tribe's lands through the U.S. court system, all efforts failed and he was forced to relocate west along with his people. His wife of many years, Quatie, died of pneumonia during the Trail of Tears after she gave her only blanket to a sick child. The next morning soldiers helped bury her in a shallow grave beside the trail.

Ross remained as leader of his tribe and guided the

reestablishment of the Cherokee Nation in the West. For the next twenty-eight years until his death, he held the tribe together, leading them through the Civil War and fighting off renewed attempts to gain land by white homesteaders. A resolution passed by the Cherokee Nation at Ross's death memorialized the faithful chief as one who "never faltered in supporting what he believed to be right, but clung to it with a steadiness of purpose which alone could have sprung from the clearest convictions of rectitude." Today he is remembered as the Moses and the George Washington of the Cherokee Nation.

SEQUOYAH, ALSO KNOWN AS GEORGE GIST, CREATED A WRITTEN LANGUAGE FOR THE CHEROKEE IN THE NINETEENTH CENTURY.

Cherokee mother. Some accounts report that Sequoyah's father was a Dutch or German peddler named Gist; others say his grandfather was a white man and his father was half Cherokee. Born around the time of the American Revolution, Sequoyah served under Andrew Jackson and fought as a member of the U.S. forces against the Creek during the War of 1812. Although he could not read or write English (or any other language), Sequoyah came to understand the value of a written language while watching other soldiers read letters and reports. After the war he returned home to eastern Tennessee and devoted the next years to creating a written Cherokee language. Eventually he created eighty-five symbols, each representing a sound, which could be combined to express concepts and thoughts. In 1821, twelve years after beginning the project, Sequoyah and his daughter began teaching the language to the Cherokee people. Four years later the Cherokee, many of whom had converted to Christianity, were reading the Bible and other religious material in their own language. In 1828 the nation published the *Cherokee Phoenix*, the first bilingual newspaper in the United States.

According to the 1825 census, 15,000 Cherokee—with their 1,300 slaves—lived on about 7 million acres of tribal lands in central Georgia, Tennessee, Alabama, North Carolina, and South Carolina. The most prosperous of the Five Civilized Tribes, the Cherokee owned 22,000 head of cattle, seven hundred looms, two thousand spinning wheels, and hundreds of plows. Gristmills, cotton gins, and sawmills manufactured goods for the tribe's own use and to sell. Many of the Cherokee married American settlers and as a result had English names. Some tribe members still practiced the old ways, but the majority lived much the same as the white settlers around them.

No doubt members of the five southern tribes considered themselves as civilized as their white counterparts. Adopting American ways, however, proved to be of little help in protecting the tribes from land fever. Through thirteen treaties negotiated with the Creek and the Cherokee, the United States took over about 15 million acres of tribal lands in Georgia between 1802 and 1819.

LIFE IN NEW ECHOTA

Everyday life in New Echota mirrored that of the tribe's Georgian neighbors. Residents lived in neat, well-maintained homes on the outskirts of town. On council meeting days, people on horses, in carriages, or on foot crowded the streets of the capital. The town had been laid out by Cherokee surveyors and boasted a sixty-foot-wide main street and a two-acre town square. In the center of town, the offices of the *Cherokee Phoenix* newspaper, the Supreme Court building, the Council House (legislature), and other government buildings lined the main street. Businesses, a ferry, and a mission center where minister Samuel Worcester lived occupied surrounding areas.

Inhabitants read the Bible and the weekly paper, attended church services, voted for legislators, and took complaints to court for a judge and jury to resolve. The wealthy rode to town in fancy carriages. Others rode horses or walked to their destinations. Children learned to read and write in the local school. Many lived on prosperous plantations, where African slaves tended the crops or performed household chores. Others worked as blacksmiths, storekeepers, and at a number of trades necessary for a prosperous nineteenth-century town.

The state of Georgia asked for federal help in persuading the Indians to cede their land, but both tribes refused to part with any more territory and even made it a capital crime for an individual Indian to sell tribal lands. Those who wanted tribal land justified their goal by maintaining that American Indians could not be "civilized" and were blocking the nation's advancement. Chief Shulush Homa of the Choctaw provided a telling commentary on white man's "civilization" in an 1824 letter to Secretary of War John C. Calhoun:

> It has been a great many years since our white brothers came across the big waters and a great many of them [have] not got civilized yet; therefore we wish to be indulged in our savage state of life until we can have the same time to get civilized . . . [and] for that reason we think we might as well enjoy our right as well as our white brothers.

state v. tribe

With the exception of a few small parcels of land in Alabama, most of the Indian territory in Alabama and Mississippi had been ceded to the United States through treaties and other means. Despite the Creek ban against land sales, Georgia officials coerced three Creek leaders into signing away much of the tribe's territory in that state with a treaty at Indian Springs in 1825. President John Quincy Adams objected and at one point sent federal troops to stop the state from surveying the land. Georgia claimed the states had as much power as the federal government to regulate the land, but the issue was left unresolved. After land originally belonging to Creek tribes was parceled out through lotteries conducted in 1821 and 1827, Georgians turned a hungry eye to the Cherokee Nation's territory. A song of the time reflected their intentions:

All I ask in this creation
Is a pretty little wife and a big plantation
Way up yonder in the Cherokee Nation.

In 1828 gold was discovered on tribal land. The news
brought more than two thousand gold seekers surging into
the area in 1829 and further ignited Georgia's lust for
Indian territory. State and federal officials did nothing to
stop the adventurers from trespassing on Cherokee property.

Beginning in the late 1820s Georgia passed a series of
laws giving the state power over the Cherokee and abol-
ishing their government and independence. On
December 20, 1828, Georgia legislators passed a law that
disbanded the Cherokee Nation's government and voided
tribal customs and laws. The only official function left to
the Cherokee was the signing of treaties. The law also
divided Cherokee land among five Georgia counties and
put the tribe under the jurisdiction of the state. The following December the state legislature passed additional
laws regulating the Cherokee Nation.

Outraged at Georgia's actions, the Cherokee and their
supporters petitioned Congress and published appeals in
the *Cherokee Phoenix* and other papers seeking justice
from the American people. A delegation of Cherokee
leaders appealed to President John Quincy Adams to
uphold the terms of previous treaties that guaranteed
their status as a nation. Adams, in the last days of his term
of office, left the matter to be decided by the incoming
president, Andrew Jackson. Jackson's answer chilled New
Echota leaders: he ordered the tribe to abide by Georgia's
rules or establish a new settlement in the West. The federal government, it was clear, would not take any action to
force Georgia to abide by the treaty terms. Jackson's
stance was contrary to that of the presidents before him.

All had supported the right of the Indians to exist as separate nations, exempt from the control of the states. Jackson, however, viewed the tribes as roadblocks to America's progress and development. He believed "civilized" white settlers would improve the land and further the nation's progress.

States' rights advocates claimed that it was up to individual states to govern those within their borders (including the Cherokee and other tribes). These proponents claimed that states had the right to overrule federal laws and national treaties. Although Jackson was no champion of states' rights, his views on the Cherokee matter put him squarely on the side of Georgia in the state's efforts to seize tribal lands.

Georgia decreed that the state would take over control of the Cherokee government on June 1, 1830. By that time Congress had passed the Indian Removal Act, which provided lands west of the Mississippi in exchange for the territory occupied by the eastern tribes. The Cherokee turned to the only avenue they had left: the U.S. Supreme Court. This set the stage for one of the greatest challenges to the Court and the U.S. Constitution.

TWO
HISTORY OF TRIBES
IN AMERICA

WHEN EXPLORER CHRISTOPHER Columbus "discovered" America, millions of people already lived in the
territories that almost three centuries later would become
the United States of America. According to some esti-
mates, 10 to 15 million natives resided in North America
in 1492. Most of the tribes dwelled along the coasts and the
fertile river valleys dotting the continent. These groups of
people—separate nations—embraced their own cultures
and customs. Each tribe spoke its own language or
dialect—approximately 550 in all—and held complex spir-
itual beliefs that governed the lives of all tribe members.
In most of the native communities, members shared food
and wealth, and every person had a job to do.

Columbus, who had hoped to land in India, called the
tribes "Indians," and the name stuck, even though it
quickly became obvious that the ships had not hit their
Asian target. Members of the indigenous people referred
to themselves by their tribal names, Cherokee, Apache,
Iroquois, and others. The earliest tribes had probably
lived on the continent for 15,000 years.

Traders were among the first Europeans to make con-
tact with North America's indigenous people. These
adventurous merchants, mostly French, swapped guns,
horses, whiskey, metal tools, and trinkets for the pelts and

furs provided by Indian hunters and in demand among fashionable Europeans. Explorers and adventurers in search of gold and other valuable resources followed.

The European visitors had a dramatic impact on the tribes, bringing death and disease to people who had never been exposed to mumps, measles, smallpox, and other illnesses. With no immunity to the European diseases, millions died. By the early 1600s when the first wave of European settlers arrived, only about 2 million Indians—about one-fifth of the original population—remained in North America.

Actually the first English settlers came to North America in 1584 and established a colony at Roanoke Island (in present-day North Carolina) the following year. Colonists dispatched to England for supplies found the settlement deserted upon their return, a mysterious "lost colony" whose fate has never been uncovered. Other colonies, however, soon took hold and flourished, including Jamestown, Virginia, in 1607 and Plymouth, Massachusetts, in 1620.

The adventurers who landed on Jamestown Island on May 14, 1607, almost immediately encountered hostile members of the Algonquin tribe. The immigrants built a fort to protect themselves and struggled to survive in the face of sickness, famine, and Indian attacks. The Algonquin chief, Powhatan, saw the English as good trading partners and swapped food for tools. His daughter Pocahontas later married Englishman John Rolfe, the first recorded marriage between a European and an American Indian.

Pilgrims landing in the North in 1620 had a brief skirmish with a small group of Indians in Cape Cod and decided to look elsewhere for a suitable place to settle. They eventually claimed a deserted village nearby that had been occupied by the Wampanoag tribe before a plague brought by European traders wiped out every inhabitant. William Bradford, a Pilgrim leader and later governor of the colony, noted in his journal that the chosen site had "neither man, woman, nor child remaining, . . . so that there is none to hinder our possession or to lay claim unto it."

"LAND CANNOT BE SOLD"

The Indian tribes' view of land and land ownership differed significantly from that of the European settlers. While distinct tribes controlled land that had been occupied by their ancestors and drove enemies from the territory, American Indians had no concept of individual land ownership. Buying and selling land was not part of Indian culture. The tribe as a group used the land to survive, then moved on as their needs and the season dictated. Two centuries later, in 1833, Black Hawk, the Sauk leader who led a rebellion against efforts to move Indians west, commented on this concept of the land:

> My reason teaches me that land cannot be sold. The Great Spirit gave it to his children to live upon and cultivate as far as necessary for their subsistence, and so long as they occupy and cultivate it they have the right to the soil, but if they voluntarily leave it, then any other people have a right to settle on it. Nothing can be sold but such things as can be carried away.

The settlers, both in Virginia and in New England, claimed ownership of the land based on charters issued in England. In 1606 King James I granted a British stock company exclusive rights to North American territory along the Atlantic seaboard. Two branches of the company oversaw the development of the land by English colonists:

American Indian warriors attack settlers at Jamestown, Virginia, around 1608. By the 1830s, settlers' demands for land had forced most

EASTERN TRIBES TO MOVE FROM THEIR TRADITIONAL HOMELANDS TO TERRI-
TORY WEST OF THE MISSISSIPPI RIVER.

the Virginia Company of London (the London Company) supervised the southern territory from North Carolina to Long Island Sound, while the Virginia Company of Plymouth (Plymouth Company) distributed land in the northern regions from Chesapeake Bay to the Canadian border. The Council for New England, which took over the land grants of the Plymouth Company after that firm closed, obtained a "sea to sea" grant from King James in 1620. The charter included all territory from the Atlantic Ocean to the Pacific Ocean that fell between the fortieth and the forty-eighth latitude north (approximately from New York to the U.S.-Canadian border).

Other land grants, issued by subsequent kings and governments, carved up additional territory in North America. During this time the French government laid claim to much of the same land chartered by the English. Spanish and Dutch explorers also put in their own claims for overlapping territory. None of the European powers even considered the land rights of the native people.

territorial disputes

The huge gap between the tribal view of communal land and the settlers' insistence on land ownership led to two centuries of territorial disputes, sometimes marked by violence. Tribes signed treaty after treaty to protect the dwindling acreage they controlled. Even though the formal treaties were instruments of the Europeans—drawn up to further their view of land ownership—the white men who signed the documents more often than not ignored the terms they had negotiated with the tribes. In the first of many such treaties, the New England Wampanoag tribe signed a treaty with the Pilgrims in 1621 pledging peace between the people of the two nations. The pact held for more than forty years, but the tribe had to cede parcels of their land to newly arrived settlers as part of the deal. In

BLACK HAWK, A SAUK CHIEF, PROCLAIMED, "MY REASON TEACHES ME THAT
LAND CANNOT BE SOLD." DESPITE THAT VIEW, WHITE COLONISTS CONTINUED
TO NEGOTIATE DEALS TO BUY THE TRIBES' TRADITIONAL LANDS.

exchange the Wampanoag received guns and protection from the Narragansett, an enemy tribe across the bay. By the 1660s, however, thousands of settlers had overrun tribal lands and seriously depleted the wildlife on which the Indians depended. Members of weaker tribes were relegated to preserves, small areas set aside for them.

Even negotiations made in good faith, with special efforts to give Indians a fair deal, turned sour when subsequent white leaders either reinterpreted treaties or ignored them. On July 15, 1682, chiefs of the Delaware tribe signed a pact with William Penn, founder of Pennsylvania, agreeing to sell land to the settlers and pledging peace. Penn, a Quaker, had a reputation among the tribes as an honorable man. Seeking permission from all the tribes before buying the land, Penn told the chiefs, "We are met on the broad pathway of good faith and good will, so that no advantage is to be taken on either side, but all to be openness, brotherhood, and love."

One deed Penn supposedly drew up in 1686 described the northern boundary of the purchased land as being "as far as a Man can go in one Day and a half [eighteen hours]." For fifty years no formal boundary existed, but settlers moved into the area in northeastern Pennsylvania. When they began to encroach on land still claimed by the tribes, Penn's sons Thomas and John and other colony officials met in 1737 with tribal representatives and signed a treaty known as the Walking Purchase, which established the land's boundaries. The Penns arranged for runners to mark the course and cleared a path through the brush. On the day of the walk, organizers along the route gave the runners food and water and provided horses to carry them across rivers. At the end of the long race the one remaining runner collapsed at the fork of the Lehigh and Delaware rivers, approximately 65 miles from the starting line. As a result, the tribes had to turn over 1,200 square miles of territory, about double the amount they had expected. When the Delaware protested against the way the walk had been conducted and refused to leave the land, the Penns persuaded an opposing tribe, the Iroquois, to drive them from the territory. The 1686 treaty has never been found, and strong evidence suggests that the Penns or other officials cheated the Indians out of land by changing or destroying the pact, if it ever existed.

Despite widespread fraud, American Indians continued to sign treaties as an ever-increasing population of white settlers scrambled for land. Often they had no choice, forced to negotiate to protect at least a portion of the territory. In some cases greedy chiefs or those posing as chiefs signed away land in exchange for gifts, payments, and special treatment for themselves and their families. In other cases colonial leaders used military force to quell tribal protests and force the chiefs to sign pacts ceding traditional Indian grounds.

ALLY or Enemy?

Throughout the later 1600s and into the mid–1700s control over North America teetered between the French and the English. Although the tribes generally tried to avoid the conflict, they often sided with one faction or the other in exchange for protection or to exact revenge against enemies on the other side. Both the French and the English recognized the value of American Indian allies and made an effort to win their allegiance. Delegations of Indians sailed to Europe, where diplomats in Paris and London wined and dined them and treated them as celebrities. A *New York Times* article reported the 1762 visit of three Cherokee chiefs—referred to as "royal representatives"—to London, where they had an audience with King George. Two army officers who had served in America acted as translators. According to the news article, the chiefs "behaved with remarkable decency and mildness." One wore "a blue mantle covered with lace" and a silver collar around his neck; the other two were clad "in scarlet, richly adorned with gold lace and silver gorgets [collars]." Hundreds gathered to greet the chiefs as they toured the city and attended the theater.

The end of the French and Indian War in 1763 brought victory for Britain and control over all land east of the Mississippi River except New Orleans and two small islands in St. Lawrence Bay. France ceded its lands west of the Mississippi as well as New Orleans to Spain in gratitude for its help during the war in Europe. France's Indian allies received nothing. The tribes on both sides lost the advantages that came from playing one European power against another.

During the dozen years leading to the American Revolution, the British exerted control over Indian lands in the east. Two superintendents oversaw Indian affairs, one for southern tribes and one for northern tribes. Although the British government considered the tribes separate nations not under the control of the colonies, it claimed jurisdiction over Indian land based on the king's charters granted in previous centuries. For a time the Royal Proclamation of October 7, 1763, issued by England's King George III, blocked land-hungry colonists from settling in the fertile lands west of the Appalachian Mountains. The proclamation set aside that area as Indian Territory and barred private land sales with Indians. This edict did not sit well with the rebellious colonists, whose grievances against the mother country had mounted rapidly. The colonies wanted control over their own affairs, including land occupied by the tribes. From 1763 to 1775 the British and the various tribes negotiated boundaries for Indian territory from Florida to Lake Ontario. Ignoring the pacts, colonists continued to push into western Pennsylvania and other areas of the Ohio River Valley. The encroachment sparked a war between settlers and the Delaware and Shawnee tribes. The Iroquois in the North, allies of the Shawnee, negotiated peace between the colonies and the tribes.

TAKING THE "VERY GROUND UNDER OUR FEET"

In October 1768, 3,400 members of the Iroquois Nation and their allies held a conference with colonial officials at Fort Stanwix in Rome, New York, to establish new boundaries for Indian territory. Bowing to the angry demands of colonists, England had abandoned the Royal Proclamation of 1763 and agreed to open the eastern and southern sections of the Ohio River Valley to white settlers. In exchange, officials promised the tribes a large parcel of land to the west of the Ohio River and north to the Canadian border. The English argued that the new territory would create a buffer between the colonists and the Indians and help preserve land for the tribes.

The chiefs wore their finest garments on this day of pageantry. The English brought gifts, hunting supplies, and goods manufactured in England. They also carried a secret stash of presents that would go to the chiefs who agreed to sign the land deal. Persuaded that the new treaty would keep settlers away from their territory and lured by the bountiful gifts, tribal leaders agreed to sell 1.8 million acres of land to the English. On November 5, 1768, they signed the Treaty of Fort Stanwix, which turned over to the British a vast tract of land running from the Mohawk River in central New York to the mouth of the Tennessee River in Kentucky. Almost immediately thousands of settlers poured into the region, gobbling up land for homesteads in what would become the states of New York, Pennsylvania, West Virginia, and Kentucky. According to one report, the Penn family received offers from 2,790 eager buyers within hours of putting on the market a parcel of land they had acquired through the treaty.

The treaty displaced several tribes who did not agree to the terms, including the Delaware, the Mingo, and the Shawnee. One tribe forced to leave their homeland had not realized the extent of the land deal until after the treaty had been signed. The Mohawk, one of the Iroquois tribes, had to share land with the Oneida in western New York. "Our lands," members of the tribe reported, "are all claimed by the white people, even the village where we reside; the very ground under our feet." The British did, however, attempt to keep settlers from infringing on the new Indian territory, which the colonists fiercely resented.

Farther south, white homesteaders and land specula-tors continued their encroachment onto Indian lands. Attorney Richard Henderson and eight investors formed the Transylvania Company in 1775 and arranged a private deal with several Cherokee chiefs to buy a huge tract of land that encompassed most of Kentucky, central Tennessee, and other territory owned by Virginia. The Transylvania Purchase, as the deal became known, was the largest private real estate transaction in the history of the United States—more than 20 million acres in all. With the deal already in place, Henderson's group made a show of meeting with more than 12,000 tribal members in a festive weeks-long conference to win their approval of the land sale. The buyers offered the Cherokee two thousand pounds sterling (worth about $344,500 in U.S. money in 2006) and eight thousand pounds (about $1,378,000 in 2006) in merchan-dise. (This would amount to about $11 an acre in 2006 money.) For another two thousand pounds' worth of goods, the tribe sold the Henderson group a path leading to the lands through the Cumberland Gap.

The disputed land had for decades served as the primary

hunting grounds for the Cherokee. Two chiefs, Dragging Canoe (Oconistoto) and Raven (Doublehead) strongly objected to the sale. Without the unanimous consent of the chiefs, the land sale was not legal under Cherokee law. Nevertheless the Indians gathered at the conference approved the sale, persuaded by the offer of goods and the encouragement of Transylvania employees such as Daniel Boone. On March 17, 1775, as the chiefs prepared to sign the Treaty of Sycamore Shoals, deeding much of Kentucky and central Tennessee to white settlers, Dragging Canoe rose in protest. His words eerily predicted the fate that awaited the Cherokee and the other eastern tribes:

> Whole Indian nations have melted away like snow-balls in the sun before the white man's advance. . . . Where are the Delawares? They have been reduced to a mere shadow of their former greatness. We had hoped that the white men would not be willing to travel beyond the mountains. Now that hope is gone. They have passed the mountains, and have settled upon Tsalagi (Cherokee) land. They wish to have that action sanctioned by treaty. When that is gained, the same encroaching spirit will lead them upon other land of the Tsalagi (Cherokee). New cessions will be asked. Finally the whole country, which the Tsalagi (Cherokee) and their fathers have so long occupied, will be demanded, and the remnant of Ani-Yunwiya, the real people, once so great and formidable, will be compelled to seek refuge in some distant wilderness. There they will be permitted to stay only a short while, until they again behold the advancing banners of the same greedy host. Not being able to point out any further retreat for the miserable Tsalagi (Cherokee), the extinction of the whole race will be proclaimed.

The British king and the governors of Virginia and North Carolina issued proclamations declaring the sale invalid. British and colonial law prohibited white men from buying land from Indians without permission from the colonial governor and council. The "vacant" land, according to the British, fell under a royal charter and would at some point be divided into lots and put up for public sale. Colonial officials also feared that the deal would spark trouble with the Indians, who had obtained a considerable amount of gunpowder as part of the exchange. The Henderson group ignored the proclamations, and settlers eager to buy land soon flooded the area. The Americans, who took over the government as a result of the Revolutionary War, held mixed views on the land sale. In 1778 the Virginia House of Delegates declared the Transylvania Purchase void but offered Henderson and his company payment for their "trouble and expense" in arranging the deal. The delegates noted that the transaction likely brought "great advantage" to the commonwealth "by increasing its inhabitants, and establishing a barrier against the Indians."

american revolution

Tensions between the colonists and the English reached a flash point in December 1773 when Boston residents threw crates of English tea into the harbor rather than pay a tax on the drink. Other ports staged their own protests, and on April 19, 1775, rebels lined up at the town square in Lexington, Massachusetts, and "fired the shot heard 'round the world." British troops sent to confiscate the rebels' guns fired back, and war erupted. The rebellious Americans issued their Declaration of Independence from England on July 4, 1776.

At first the Americans counseled the Indians to remain neutral. The British, however, sought alliances with the tribes, and most either joined the loyalist cause or tried to stay out of the war. The Iroquois threw their support to the British, whose forts offered protection against attack from settlers intent on taking Indian land. The British also offered payment and goods in trade for tribal aid. In addition the sister of the powerful Mohawk chief Joseph Brant had married William Johnson, the British superintendent of Indians. As the war progressed, American leaders sought the help of the Indians, but most of the tribes turned down their requests. Several northern tribes, including the Mohawk, persuaded the Cherokee and the Creek to take up arms against the Americans. When the Cherokee attacked along the frontier, American freedom fighters leveled their villages, and the tribe retreated west.

Thomas Jefferson was incensed at the actions of the Cherokee. In a letter to a friend in August 1776, he wrote:

> I hope the Cherokees will now be driven beyond the Mississippi & that this in future will be declared to the Indians the invariable conse-quence of their beginning a war. Our contest with Britain is too serious and too great to permit any possibility of avocation from the Indians. This then is the season for driving them off. . . .

Jefferson also noted that the Six Nations of the Iro-quois tribes "immediately changed their conduct" after being warned that if they did not remain neutral in the war, "we [Americans] would never cease waging war with them while one was to be found on the face of the earth."

Despite Jefferson's assurances to the contrary, many tribes fought fiercely for the British throughout the Revo-lution. In the North, Chief Brant of the Mohawk distin-guished himself as a brilliant strategist who convinced

THE SIX NATIONS

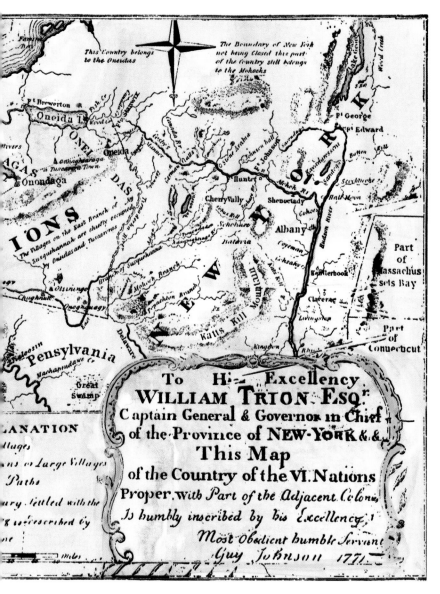

THIS MAP, CREATED AT THE DIRECTION OF THE BRITISH IN 1771, DEPICTS THE
TERRITORY CLAIMED BY THE SIX NATIONS IN NEW YORK, PENNSYLVANIA, AND
THE GREAT LAKES REGION. THE CONFEDERACY WAS COMPRISED OF SIX
NORTHERN TRIBES, THE MOHAWK, THE CAYUGA, THE SENECA, THE ONEIDA,
THE ONONDAGA, AND THE TUSCARORA.

four of the Six Nations to join the British in the war. The Oneida and the Tuscarora broke ranks with the Iroquois Confederacy and fought with the Americans in an unsuccessful attempt to free Fort Stanwix from British control in 1777. Many Indians on both sides lost their lives in the ensuing battle. In 1780 two thousand Creek helped the British defend Pensacola (Florida) from Spanish forces allied with the Americans. The following March a much larger Spanish fleet overpowered the British and their Creek and Choctaw allies. With that defeat, the Cherokee and the Chickasaw chose to make peace with the Americans, but the Creek remained firmly in the British camp. The Choctaw came to no decision on which course to follow.

Some tribes eventually joined forces with the rebels. Both the Indians and their American allies wanted to throw off the yoke of British control over the lands along the Ohio Valley. Ultimately, though, the land claims would pit the former allies against one another—and the Americans would win.

peace and promises broken

When the war ended in 1783, the tribes faced retribution from the victorious Americans and received little help from their British allies. During peace negotiations in France the defeated English surrendered claim to all lands east of the Mississippi River. The formal Peace of Paris, signed on September 3, 1783, completely ignored Indian claims to their traditional lands, including the northeastern Indian Territory, which the British had guaranteed to the Indians a decade and a half earlier under the Treaty of Fort Stanwix.

The treaty's terms infuriated Indian leaders. Brant, in particular, had expected the English to defend Indian claims. The tribes' supporters, among them Daniel Claus, Britain's superintendent of Indians in Canada, shared Brant's outrage. The peace treaty, he said, might have

SIX NATIONS CONFEDERACY

For many centuries, five tribes in the northeastern region of North America—Mohawk, Cayuga, Seneca, Oneida, and Onondaga—had joined together in a loose association and followed a democratic form of government. When the Tuscarora joined the alliance in the early 1700s the league became known as the Six Nations, or the Iroquois Confederacy. All the tribes shared the Iroquois language.

Each tribe retained its independence and identity within the larger confederation. The Great Council Fire, the governing body of the league, consisted of representatives from all six tribes. Council members were men selected by the head woman in each clan. Members served life terms and met yearly to discuss strategies and plan the league's activities.

The league's Great Law of Peace—the confederacy's unwritten constitution—stipulated that decisions would be made democratically, with all nations allotted time to discuss the matter at hand and each tribe given an equal say:

> Then shall the Onondaga chiefs declare the Council open. . . . All the business . . . shall be conducted by the two combined bodies of Confederate chiefs. First the question shall be passed upon by the Mohawk and Seneca chiefs, then it shall be discussed and passed by the Oneida and Cayuga chiefs. Their decision shall then be referred to the Onondaga chiefs, the Firekeepers, for final judgment.

The Tuscarora would later be included in the discussions. Major actions required the approval of all six tribes. Council members who misbehaved or did not properly represent their tribe could be impeached, or removed from office. Within each tribe, government followed a similar pattern. Each village had a council made up of the wise elders of the tribe. Often the wisest or most able person was chosen as chief; sometimes the position was inherited. Before making important decisions the chief consulted with the council. Women and younger men were also included in the discussion. Chiefs rarely made decisions on their own.

Benjamin Franklin, Thomas Jefferson, George Washington, and other American founders were familiar with the Iroquois Confederacy and used it as one of their models when drawing up the U.S. Constitution and establishing a democratic government. In the twentieth century the United Nations would adopt many of the same concepts embraced by the Iroquois tribes.

In 1915 Arthur C. Parker, archaeologist for the New York State Museum, transcribed the Iroquois constitution from the oral version that had been passed down over the centuries. After more than eight hundred years, the confederacy continues as the oldest participatory democracy in the world.

easily stipulated "that those lands the Crown relinquished to all the Indian Nations as their Right and property were out of its [England's] power to treat for." The Spanish agent at the Paris treaty conference, Pedro Pablo Abarca de Bolea, the count of Aranda, was even blunter. "Free and independent nations of Indians" had claim to the lands that lay between the Appalachian Mountain chain and the Mississippi River, he said. "You have no right to it," he told the English, but they ceded the land to the Americans anyway.

Britain's prime minister, William Petty, Earl of Shelburne, had no such qualms. Defending the terms of the treaty, he contended that "the Indian nations were not abandoned to their enemies; they were remitted to the care of neighbours." Some English officials believed the Indian Territory in the Northeast would serve as a useful buffer between the new American nation and British-owned Canada and thus supported the tribes' claims.

But American negotiators led by John Jay insisted that the United States maintain control over Indian land as a condition of the treaty. "With respect to the Indians," Jay asserted, "we claim the right of preemption; with respect to all other nations, we claim the sovereignty over the territory." The Americans, he stated, would not honor other nations' treaties with the tribes. Jay and others considered Indians to be allies of the British, and as such, a defeated people with no rights to America's land.

Ostensibly, Congress followed a more moderate course when it passed the Northwest Ordinance of 1787. As part of the act Congress promised to respect the land rights of the tribes:

> The utmost good faith shall always be observed towards the Indians; their lands and their property shall never be taken from them without their consent; and in their property, rights and liberty, they

shall never be invaded or disturbed, unless in just and lawful wars authorized by Congress.

The main thrust of the ordinance, however, established guidelines for creating new states in a vast region to the north where many Indian tribes resided. The parcel covered nearly 170 million acres of prime farmland bounded by the Mississippi River to the west, the Ohio River to the south and east, and the Great Lakes to the north. Eventually the states of Ohio, Michigan, Indiana, Illinois, and Wisconsin would occupy the territory. The ordinance further encouraged white settlement in the area by requiring a population of 60,000 before a region could become a state. Under the influence of Rufus King, an ardent abolitionist and one of the principal authors of the ordinance, slavery was banned in the territory.

War expenses amassed during the American Revolution had put the new nation in debt and threatened its economy. Leaders saw public land sales as one way to bring money into national coffers. The pressure to acquire land—by state and federal governments as well as settlers and land speculators—further eroded tribal holdings. Making matters worse for the tribes, many Americans still harbored hostility against them for siding with the British during the war and attacking frontier homes.

In 1784 leaders of the new American nation renegotiated the Fort Stanwix treaty, whittling away more Indian land in western New York and northwest of the Ohio River. During those dealings James Duane, a U.S. treaty agent and delegate to the first Congress, counseled George Clinton, governor of New York, to disregard the tribes' claims of being separate nations:

Instead of conforming to Indian political behavior, we should force them to adopt ours. I would never suffer the word "Nation" or "Six Nations," or "Confederates," or "Council Fire at Onondaga" or any other form which would revive or seem to confirm their former ideas of independence . . . they are used to [being] called Brethren, Sachems, and Warriors of the Six Nations. I hope it will never be repeated. . . . They should rather be taught . . . that the public opinion of their importance has long ceased.

Duane's words set the stage for the travesty that occurred at Fort Stanwix. According to historian Alvin Josephy Jr. in his book *500 Nations*, U.S. delegates to the treaty conference "seized Iroquois hostages and conducted negotiations literally at gunpoint, threatened military action against women and children in the Iroquois villages, and treated Indian spokesmen in an arbitrary, high-handed manner, intentionally insulting them and threatening a continuation of the war against them."

Under that treaty and a second one made in 1788 between New York State and the Iroquois, the Indians ceded a total of 8 million acres. Forced to abandon their homelands, the tribes settled in a much smaller area in New York reserved for them.

In the years that followed, tribes occupying lands along the Great Lakes and the Ohio Valley ceded millions of acres to the U.S. government. Few of these deals were negotiated in "good faith" as stipulated in the Ordinance of 1787. As they had done at Fort Stanwix, U.S. agents bribed, bullied, and threatened chiefs into signing treaties disadvantageous to their people. Ample supplies of rum and whiskey brought to the treaty conferences by the Americans made it easier to cheat the tribes of their land. Typical of the deals was one made with the Seneca of Pennsylvania and ratified in the Treaty of Fort Harmar in 1789. Under the terms of the pact, the tribe received about six thousand dollars, or three cents an acre, for more than 200,000 acres of land along Lake Erie. Congress later sold the land to the state of Pennsylvania for $151,640.

Nineteenth-century historian Henry Adams aptly described the effect these treaties had on the tribes as land acquisitions by white settlers ate into the fabric of Indian life:

> No acid ever worked more mechanically on a vegetable fibre than the white man acted on the Indian. As the line of American settlements approached, the nearest Indian tribes withered away.

The Americans may have considered the Indians a conquered people, but the tribes believed otherwise. Pushed into ever smaller parcels farther and farther from their traditional lands, the tribes rebelled. During the summer of 1788, tribes led raids on settlements all along the frontier. American forces led by Brigadier General Josiah Harmar met with defeat in 1790 at the hands of Indian warriors to the north. The following year Little Turtle, a chief of the Miami, and Blue Jacket of the Shawnee orchestrated a staggering defeat of U.S. troops camped along the Wabash River in the heart of Indian country. With hatchets and knives, the warriors killed 630 soldiers and wounded another 283. Only 21 Indians lost their lives in the battle, the worst defeat of the army by Indians in the nation's history. Tecumseh, a young Shawnee who would later lead his own battle against the English, participated in the rout. The settlers clamored for war against the Indians. For a time it appeared as if the British along the Canadian border would assist in the Indian cause. But when well-trained army troops under

General "Mad" Anthony Wayne drove the Indians toward Fort Miami, the British locked the gates against the retreating warriors. The conflict ended with yet another treaty in which the tribes lost more land and the Americans broke promises to keep settlers out of tribal territory.

The Louisiana Purchase (outlined in brown, 1803) nearly doubled the territory of the United States. Many U.S. officials believed that shipping tribes to the new lands to the west of the Mississippi River would solve the friction between American Indians and settlers.

THREE
THE LOUISIANA PURCHASE
AND THE PUSH WEST

In 1803 THE UNITED STATES doubled its territory when it bought a vast tract of land from France. Known as the Louisiana Purchase, the territory covered more than 828,000 square miles west of the Mississippi River. The land would eventually be divided into thirteen states. This addition to U.S. holdings ignited the push westward by settlers seeking adventure and land. Many Americans considered it their right—their destiny—to claim the fertile lands that stretched before them. They believed it their duty to bring democracy and civilization to the wilderness, a concept later called manifest destiny. William Henry Harrison, governor of the Indiana Territory and later president, championed those views:

> Is one of the fairest portions of the globe to remain in a state of nature, the haunt of a few wretched savages, when it seems destined by the Creator to give support to a large population and to be the seat of civilization?

In the first decades of the 1800s homesteaders continued to stream into the valleys east of the Mississippi River, increasing the tension between the settlers and the tribes in the region. These new residents took over traditional Indian hunting grounds and destroyed habitat that supported the wild animals on which the tribes depended. A few tribes turned to farming to survive, only to lose their plots to white farmers.

Land Swap

President Thomas Jefferson saw the vast holdings acquired in the Louisiana Purchase as the answer to the settlers' problems with Indians. He suggested that tribes swap their land in the East for acreage west of the Mississippi. Jefferson no doubt viewed himself as a friend to the Indians, but his ultimate goal was to provide land for his fellow Americans and open the eastern territory to development.

Jefferson maintained that the land swap should be voluntary. He reiterated that position in 1786 when he answered questions posed to him by Monsieur de Meusnier, a French theorist who had recently written an article on politics. "It may be regarded as certain," Jefferson wrote, "that not a foot of land will ever be taken from the Indians without their own consent. The sacredness of their rights is felt by all thinking persons in America, as much as in Europe."

The tribes in the eastern part of America, however, had no desire to move from their homelands to unknown territory. Throughout the 1810s and 1820s they faced increasing pressure to leave their land. Many of the tribes migrated from one area to another depending on the season. When they returned to their territory for a new season, they found settlers had cultivated the land and built houses on the site.

William Henry Harrison did what he could to drive tribes farther west. He negotiated new treaties with tribes, giving them money, goods, and promises of yearly stipends in exchange for land for settlers. Since his defeat at Fort Miami, Tecumseh had rallied support from a dozen tribes, formed a confederation, and mustered an army of six thousand warriors. Determined to preserve Indian territory, the chief urged tribes to join his confederation and stop sales of tribal lands. In 1810 Tecumseh and his followers met with Harrison at Vincennes, the capital of Indiana Territory, to renegotiate land treaties. Both sides left the conference ready for war. In 1811 the forces met outside the Indian confederation's headquarters in northwestern Indiana near Tippecanoe River. With Tecumseh away recruiting Indian allies, his religious brother Tenskwatawa, called the Prophet, directed a surprise early-morning attack against the army. Although the Indians killed many U.S. soldiers and several key military leaders during the attack, Harrison's forces persevered and burned the abandoned Indian headquarters to the ground. The conflict gave Harrison the slogan he needed to win the presidency, "Tippecanoe and Tyler too," with John Tyler as his vice president, in 1840.

WAR OF 1812

When war broke out between Britain and the United States in 1812, Tecumseh grabbed the opportunity to win an important ally to the Indian cause. The British accepted his offer of help, made him a brigadier general, and placed him in charge of an American Indian army of 15,000 warriors. Tecumseh's brilliant maneuvers helped the British win several battles along the U.S.-Canadian border. After Americans under Commodore Oliver Hazard Perry wiped out the British fleet on Lake Erie, Harrison's forces attacked the British at the Battle of the Thames in Ontario. On October 5, 1813, an American soldier's bullet pierced Tecumseh's chest, killing him and ending the Indian confederation.

In the South, the Lower Creek, the Cherokee, and the Choctaw joined the Tennessee militia led by Andrew

TECUMSEH ORGANIZED TRIBES INTO A CONFEDERACY TO FIGHT U.S. FORCES DURING THE WAR OF 1812. SOLDIERS UNDER THE COMMAND OF WILLIAM HENRY HARRISON KILLED THE SHAWNEE LEADER DURING THE BATTLE OF THE THAMES IN ONTARIO ON OCTOBER 5, 1813.

Jackson to fight the Red Stick, an offshoot of the Upper Creek, who supported the British. During the Battle of Horseshoe Bend in 1814 the American and Indian forces killed eight hundred Red Stick. Those who remained fled to Florida. After the battle Jackson informed the Creek chiefs who had helped defeat the Red Stick that they would have to cede two-thirds of their land to the American government. They resisted but ultimately were forced to sign the Treaty of Fort Jackson agreeing to the terms. It would not be the last time Jackson betrayed Indian friends.

As the war drew to a close, it became apparent that the tribes would be the biggest losers in the conflict. The signing of the Treaty of Ghent on December 24, 1814, ended the war but essentially allowed England and the United States to continue as before. Initially British negotiators pushed, as they had after the American Revolution, for an Indian Territory to serve as a buffer between the United States and Canada. The British quickly abandoned the demand in the face of America's adamant rejection of such a proposal. By then, 100,000 settlers had moved into the territory originally set aside for Indians. Ohio had become a state in 1803, and Indiana and Illinois achieved statehood in 1816 and 1818, respectively. The American delegates said they would never agree to "abandon territory and a portion of their citizens [or] to admit a foreign interference in their domestic concerns, and to cease to exercise their natural rights on their own shores and in their own waters."

INDIAN REMOVAL ACT OF 1830

In the more than thirty years since the colonists had set up an independent nation on the North American continent, the population of the United States had skyrocketed. Settlers had pushed across the Appalachian ridge and were now pouring into the fertile valleys between the mountains

Removal ACT OF 1830

CHAP. CXLVIII.—An Act to provide for an exchange of lands with the Indians residing in any of the states or territories, and for their removal west of the river Mississippi.

Be it enacted by the Senate and House of Representatives of the United States of America, in Congress assembled, That it shall and may be lawful for the President of the United States to cause so much of any territory belonging to the United States, west of the river Mississippi, not included in any state or organized territory, and to which the Indian title has been extinguished, as he may judge necessary, to be divided into a suitable number of districts, for the reception of such tribes or nations of Indians as may choose to exchange the lands where they now reside, and remove there; and to cause each of said districts to be so described by natural or artificial marks, as to be easily distinguished from every other.

SEC. 2. And be it further enacted, That it shall and may be lawful for the President to exchange any or all of such districts, so to be laid off and described, with any tribe or nation within the limits of any of the states or territories, and with which the United States have existing treaties, for the whole or any part or portion of the territory claimed and occupied by such tribe or nation, within the bounds of any one or more of the states or territories, where the land claimed and occupied by the Indians, is owned by the United States, or the United States are bound to the state within which it lies to extinguish the Indian claim thereto.

SEC. 3. And be it further enacted, That in the making of any such exchange or exchanges, it shall and may be lawful for the President solemnly to assure the tribe or nation with which the exchange is made, that the United States will forever secure and guaranty to them, and their heirs or successors, the country so exchanged with them; and if they prefer it, that the United States will cause a patent or grant to be made and executed to them for the same: Provided always, That such lands shall revert to the United States, if the Indians become extinct, or abandon the same.

SEC. 4. And be it further enacted, That if, upon any of the lands now occupied by the Indians, and to be exchanged for, there should be such improvements as add value to the land claimed by any individual or individuals of such tribes or nations, it shall and may be lawful for the President to cause such value to be ascertained by appraisement or otherwise, and to cause such ascertained value to be paid to the person or persons rightfully claiming such improvements. And upon the payment of such valuation, the improvements so valued and paid for, shall pass to the United States, and possession shall not afterwards be permitted to any of the same tribe.

SEC. 5. And be it further enacted, That upon the making of any such exchange as is contemplated by this act, it shall and may be lawful for the President to cause such aid and assistance to be furnished to the emigrants as may be necessary and proper to enable them to remove to, and settle in, the country for which they may have exchanged; and also, to give them such aid and assistance as may be necessary for their support and subsistence for the first year after their removal.

SEC. 6. And be it further enacted, That it shall and may be lawful for the President to cause such tribe or nation to be protected, at their new residence, against all interruption or disturbance from any other tribe or nation of Indians, or from any other person or persons whatever.

SEC. 7. And be it further enacted, That it shall and may be lawful for the President to have the same superintendence and care over any tribe or nation in the country to which they may remove, as contemplated by this act, that he is now authorized to have over them at their present places of residence.

and the Mississippi River. With the acquisition of the Louisiana Purchase, adventuresome families had settled in wild lands along the Missouri River and north into the Great Lakes region. By 1820 the population of the area occupying present-day Kentucky, Tennessee, Ohio, Louisiana, Illinois, Indiana, Mississippi, and Alabama had increased to 2,216,000. Only one-sixth of those people had resided in the region in 1800. During that same two decades the total population of the United States grew from 5.3 million to 9.6 million.

The rapidly growing population demanded land. For many, that land lay in tribal territory, and the one sure way to get it was to move the tribes to the West. In 1817 the Committee on Public Lands prepared a report for the U.S. Senate on the subject. The report concluded that land east of the Mississippi should be taken from the tribes to accommodate the new settlers coming into the area. In exchange the tribes would be given comparable land in the western territory acquired as part of the Louisiana Purchase.

The report acknowledged, however, that the deal could go through only with the voluntary consent of the tribes. The government, it noted, would have to negotiate terms and sign a treaty with the Indians. "Those tribes have been recognized so far, as independent communities, as to become parties to treaties with us, and to have a right to govern themselves without being subject to the laws of the United States; and their right to remain in possession of the lands they occupy, and to sell them when they please, has been always acknowledged."

Andrew Jackson had little sympathy for Indians' rights. Jackson, in a letter to James Monroe in 1817, rejected the notion of tribes as independent entities: "I have long viewed treaties with the Indians an absurdity not to be reconciled to the principles of our government. . . .

The Indians are the subjects of the United States, inhabiting its territory and acknowledging its sovereignty."

President James Monroe supported the plan to remove eastern tribes to the West. In a letter to the Senate in 1825 Monroe wrote that the removal and "well-digested plan for their government and civilization" should be agreeable to the Indians and would "not only shield them from impending ruin, but promote their welfare and happiness." Without such a plan to address the problems that beset the tribes, they faced certain degradation and extermination, according to the president.

In the past Congress had supported, at least on paper, the right of Indians to their land. That policy came under fire when Jackson became president in 1829. Jackson, who had built a reputation as an Indian fighter, proposed that tribes be moved from their lands in the East, by force if necessary, and given an equal amount of land in what was known as the "Great American Desert" west of the Mississippi River. The new "Indian Territory," occupied a vast expanse where Americans, presumably, would not want to settle. It would later become the state of Oklahoma.

Jackson's proposal, embodied in the Indian Removal Act of 1830, sparked a four-month discussion in Congress. Some of those favoring the bill did little to disguise their contempt for the tribes. Georgia's representatives put the issue in terms of states' rights. They asked if other states would allow a foreign nation over which they had no control to occupy land within their borders. Others, including Jackson, tried to coat the proposal with a veneer of concern for the tribes' welfare. In introducing the bill to Congress at the opening of the session, Jackson urged the legislators to set aside "an ample district west of the Mississippi," where the Indians would be free to live under their own governments "having a distinct control over the portion designated for [their] use" and guaranteed to

ANDREW JACKSON, "OLD HICKORY"

Andrew Jackson, the nation's seventh president, was a complex and complicated man. He has been accused of the genocide of America's Indian tribes while also being hailed as a man of the people, the first to be elected by popular vote.

Born in 1767 in the backwoods of the Carolinas, he had little schooling. His father died before he was born. Jackson had just turned eight when the American Revolution broke out, and he was only fourteen when he and his brother Robert were captured by the British. Within the year, Robert had died from smallpox, and Jackson's mother had died of disease while tending American prisoners of war. His only other sibling, Hugh, died during a battle with the British in 1779.

The young Jackson lived with relatives for a while, worked as an apprentice making saddles, and became a teacher. In his late teens he studied law and became a lawyer in North Carolina. In 1788 he won an appointment as a prosecuting officer in the Superior Court in Nashville, a part of North Carolina at the time. A skilled lawyer, he was elected as Tennessee's first congressman when that area became a state. Jackson also operated a prosperous thousand-acre plantation, the Hermitage, where he raised cotton and had more than one hundred slaves.

Jackson and his wife, Rachel, adopted her brother's child and named him Andrew Jackson Jr. The couple also cared for a young Creek boy and several other children at the Hermitage, Jackson's Tennessee plantation. Hot-tempered, proud, and a fierce competitor, Jackson often became embroiled in disputes. In 1806 he killed a man in a duel who had made disparaging remarks about Rachel.

Staring down at an opponent with steely blue eyes peering from beneath a prominent brow, the six-foot-one-inch Jackson could intimidate the bravest of men. During the War of 1812 he led troops in several battles against the Creek and other tribes supporting the British. He became known as "Old Hickory" (an exceptionally strong wood), because of his tough, no-nonsense command over his men. During the Battle of New Orleans at the war's end General Jackson led a motley army of U.S. troops, free blacks, Indians, and frontiersmen in a decisive victory over the British redcoats. Jackson became a war hero, which led to his candidacy for president in 1824. Although Jackson won the popular vote by a decisive margin, he failed to get enough votes from the electoral college. Ultimately the House of Representatives gave the presidency to John Quincy Adams. Jackson used his popularity among the voters to build a populist party, the Democratic Party, which focused on the needs of the common people. He won an overwhelming victory in the 1828 presidential election. He was reelected in 1832.

The first westerner to hold that high office, Jackson led the country as he had his soldiers: as a tough and powerful ruler. As representative of the people, he claimed the power to override other branches of government. He vetoed more bills than all six presidents before him combined; he undermined and then shut down the powerful national bank; and he defied the U.S. Supreme Court's ruling in the *Worcester* case. Jackson also challenged the power of the states when he threatened to send in troops to force states to abide by federal laws they did not like.

Nevertheless, in the *Worcester* case Jackson's views coincided with those who championed states' rights. He and the states both believed tribal lands in the East should be turned over to "civilized" whites. While president, Jackson pursued a policy of removing eastern tribes to

U.S. President Andrew Jackson

undeveloped lands west of the Mississippi River. As a result of his removal campaign, whites took over about 100 million acres of the eastern tribes' ancestral lands. Thousands of Indians died during the removal. Jackson may have been sincere in believing that moving them to the wild country in the West would protect the tribes from annihilation, but he held no respect for the tribes' cultures. Instead he urged "superior" whites to try to "civilize" the Indians once they moved west, ignoring the Cherokee's elaborate governmental structure that practically duplicated America's own. After two terms in office, Jackson retired to the Hermitage, where he died in 1845.

them for as long as they remained there. "By promoting union and harmony among [the tribes]," Jackson said, the removal west would "perpetuate the race, and . . . attest the humanity and justice of this Government." He, like President James Monroe before him, believed that the tribes could not assimilate into white society and faced extinction if they did not leave their eastern lands for the West.

In the Senate, pro-Jackson partisans and southerners lobbied for passage of the bill. Even though the bill applied to both northern and southern tribes, southern states applied the most pressure to remove Indians from their borders. Since slavery was banned in the Northwest Territory, many in the South viewed the bill as a way to increase the holdings of slave states. John Forsyth of Georgia led supporters rallying around the bill. Referring to the tribes in his state as "a population useless and burthensome," he readily acknowledged that he believed the Indian land in his state should be prepared for "survey, sale, and settlement." If the tribes did not move, he said, they would have to abide by state laws, and "Georgia will never submit to a petty tribe of Indians."

The Whigs and anti-Jackson forces in the Northeast spoke forcefully against the bill, but they were in the minority. Senator Theodore Frelinghuysen of New Jersey asked in disgust, "Is it one of the prerogatives of the white man, that he may disregard the dictates of moral principles, where an Indian shall be concerned?" He attempted to add a provision to the bill that would protect the tribes' right to their traditional lands in the east "from all interruptions and encroachments" until they chose to leave. Later, however, in the face of the states' and Jackson's determination to move the tribes, Frelinghuysen wrote to a friend that it was probably best for the Indians to relocate west.

Representative John Bell of Tennessee, a strong

Jackson supporter and chair of the Indian Affairs Committee, shepherded the bill through the House. As in the
Senate, most opponents in the House were members of
the Whig or anti-Jackson factions, while proponents were
Jackson allies and Democrats. In the larger House, however, several representatives from the South, including
frontiersman David (Davy) Crockett of Tennessee, voted
with northerners against the Indian removal.

Representative Wilson Lumpkin of Georgia presented
a strong defense of the bill, claiming that it was "a measure
of life and death" for the tribes. "Pass the bill on your
table, and you save them. Reject it, and you leave them to
perish," he told his fellow legislators. Lumpkin, who
would later serve as Georgia's governor, argued that—even
in the face of the Cherokee settlement at Echota with its
court system and constitution— most Indians were savages
who could not be civilized. "A large portion of full blooded
Cherokee still remain a poor degraded race of human
beings," he said.

Richard Wilde, another representative from Georgia,
contended that the tribes never had claim to all the land
when Europeans first arrived in North America. They had
rights only to the land they cultivated, and that England, as
a more "civilized" nation, overrode any original rights the
"heathen Indian population" might have had.

A third Georgian representative, Henry Lamar,
warned that if the bill failed, it would lead to "misery on
the part of the unfortunate race of people." Noting the
decline of the tribes in the East, Lamar argued that they
would be better served by sending them to lands away from
the "civilized" Americans.

Other congressmen, however, suggested that the real
reasons behind the bill had more to do with greed and lust
for the land than true sympathy for the tribes. "If [I]
believed that the real object and only effort of the bill was

to further the policy of providing a country beyond the Mississippi for such of the Indian tribes as might be inclined, of their own free choice, to remove there, [I] should have cheerfully given [my] support to the measure," Representative William Storrs, a Connecticut Whig, said during debate on the matter. Since the government itself was responsible for the Indians' plight, Storrs questioned why anyone should believe that the same body would now be acting for the benefit of the tribes. He cited several treaties with the Cherokee and the Creek to illustrate his point.

In treaties of the 1790s, he noted, the United States "solemnly guarantied" to both tribes that their lands would be protected, "quieting forever the collisions which had taken place between [the tribes] and the adjoining States." Little more than a decade later, the United States had drawn up new treaties that eliminated Indian title to part of the land and transferred ownership rights to Georgia. Later President Jackson supported Georgia's move to take over all the land and put the tribes under the state's jurisdiction. Storrs charged that by his actions, Jackson had removed the tribes from the protection of the United States and nullified valid treaties without consulting Congress. Pushing the same policy, he was now pressuring Congress to pass the removal bill, Storrs said. He urged his fellow lawmakers to ignore Jackson's influence and examine the issue with fair and open minds.

Representative George Evans of Maine, a Whig who vehemently opposed the removal, went so far as to accuse Georgia of trying to "annihilate an entire population for the purpose of gaining land." He read a letter from General William Clark (who had explored the western territory with Meriwether Lewis in 1804–1806) that described tribes already living in the West as "the most pitiable that can be imagined." Members of the western tribes, Clark wrote, starved to death. Sending more tribes to the region, Evans argued, would only make the situation worse.

Several amendments were proposed. Storrs presented an amendment that would bar the occupation or sale of lands belonging to the Cherokee Nation or other Indians without their consent. Representative Joseph Hemphill proposed an even more radical amendment that would have set aside the entire bill and replaced it with a panel of disinterested commissioners who would poll the Cherokee on their views, escort members of the tribe to the proposed new settlement, and allow the tribes to make the decision whether to go or stay. In its final form the Indian Removal Act of 1830 included wording indicating that the western lands would be given to "such tribes or nations of Indians as may choose to exchange the lands where they now reside." When it came time to enforce the law, however, tribes were given no choice in the matter.

In the final days of the first session, after months of bitter debate, Congress passed the Indian Removal Act. Twenty-eight senators voted in favor of the bill, while nineteen opposed it in a roll-call vote on April 24. The vote split down party lines, with Democrats and Jackson supporters on the winning side and Whigs and anti-Jackson senators the losers. Among the supporters was John Tyler of Virginia, vice president under William Henry Harrison, and later president. The bill passed in the House by a slim five-vote margin, 102 to 97. Jackson signed the bill on May 28, 1830. At the time of the bill's passage, more than 90,000 Indians lived east of the Mississippi River, including 60,000 in the southern tribes. All were subject to removal under the terms of the bill.

"BENEVOLENT" OPPORTUNITY

At least two states had already taken measures to force tribes from their borders. In 1829 Alabama had claimed ownership of all tribal land in that state. The Mississippi legislators in March 1830 made it a crime for American Indians to practice tribal rituals within their borders. Chiefs who led such religious ceremonies could be fined and jailed. That same year Mississippi ordered Choctaw and Chickasaw out of the state and abolished "all rights, privileges, immunities, and franchises held, claimed, or enjoyed by those persons called Indians within the chartered limits of the State."

Five months after the passage of the Indian Removal Act, the Choctaw became the first tribe to formally exchange their land for acreage in the West. Choctaw chiefs signed the Treaty of Dancing Rabbit Creek on September 27, 1830, trading their eastern territory for 140,000 acres west of the Mississippi. Ultimately the tribe retained only about half that amount because of crooked land deals that turned over large parcels of the territory to speculators. Two half-white leaders of the tribe received large tracts of land along the Tennessee River for their help in convincing the tribe to agree to the deal. Almost four thousand members of the tribe died on the trip west. Many froze to death in the Oklahoma snow or starved along the trail. One observer later called the tribes' forced move "next to a system of deliberate murder." The few Choctaw who remained became the victims of white squatters who took over their land.

In his report on the progress of the Indian removal to Congress on December 6, 1830, Jackson portrayed the upheaval in paternalistic and unrealistically optimistic terms. He announced that the "benevolent policy of the Government . . . in relation to the removal of the Indians beyond the white settlements" was nearing "a happy consummation." Two tribes had agreed to move west, and Jackson hoped their decision would "induce the remaining tribes also to seek the same obvious advantages." Many of

Captives Black Hawk, a Sauk chief (wearing a turban), and Wabo-kieshiek (White Cloud), also called the Winnebago Prophet, meet with President Andrew Jackson in Washington, D.C., in 1833 after the defeat of the Sauk and the Fox at the end of the Black Hawk War. The tribes fought unsuccessfully to stay on their tribal lands in Wisconsin and Illinois.

the advantages he cited, however, benefited white settlers. The removal of the tribes, Jackson said, would:

> • allow a "civilized population" to inhabit land "now occupied by a few savage hunters";
> • strengthen the southwestern frontier and allow southern states to "repel future invasions";
> • "relieve" Mississippi and western Alabama of "Indian occupancy" and enable the two states "to advance rapidly in population, wealth, and power."

According to Jackson, the move would help Indians by keeping the tribes away from white settlers and free of state control. It would also slow the "decay" that had reduced the numbers of Indians in the East and perhaps lead them eventually "to cast off their savage habits and become an interesting, civilized, and Christian community." The tribes' "savage habits" seemed incomprehensible to Jackson:

> What good man would prefer a country covered with forests and ranged by a few thousand savages to our extensive Republic, studded with cities, towns, and prosperous farms embellished with all the improvements which art can devise or industry execute, occupied by more than 12,000,000 happy people, and filled with all the blessings of liberty, civilization and religion?

In concluding his address, Jackson painted the tribes' "opportunity" to move in rosy terms. Many Americans happily left their ancestral homes and moved at their own expense to new lands. He noted they would be filled with "gratitude and joy" if they were offered the deal given to the Indians—an all-expense-paid trip to the West with large parcels of land provided by the government. "How many thousands of our own people would gladly embrace the opportunity of removing to the West on such conditions!"

THE CASE

OF

THE CHEROKEE NATION

against

THE STATE OF GEORGIA:

ARGUED AND DETERMINED AT

THE SUPREME COURT OF THE UNITED STATES,

JANUARY TERM 1831.

WITH

AN APPENDIX,

Containing the Opinion of Chancellor Kent on the Case; the Treaties between
the United States and the Cherokee Indians; the Act of Congress of
1802, entitled 'An Act to regulate intercourse with the Indian
tribes, &c.'; and the Laws of Georgia relative to the
country occupied by the Cherokee Indians,
within the boundary of that State.

BY RICHARD PETERS,

COUNSELLOR AT LAW.

Philadelphia:

JOHN GRIGG, 9 NORTH FOURTH STREET.

1831.

four
TO THE SUPREME COURT

AS THE nation's HIGHEST Tribunal, the Supreme Court is responsible for ruling on disputes involving treaties, deciding conflicts between state laws and the federal government, and acting as a final appeals court. In March 1831 the Cherokee petitioned the Supreme Court seeking protection from the acts passed by the Georgia legislature in 1828 and 1829. John Sergeant, representing the Cherokee, asked the Supreme Court to issue an injunction to prevent the state from seizing Cherokee lands and destroying the tribe's political system. The tribe hoped the justices would require Georgia to abide by the terms of the treaties, which guaranteed Cherokee rights as a sovereign nation. William Wirt, former U.S. attorney general, argued the case for the Cherokee before the Supreme Court. The case, *Cherokee Nation* v. *Georgia*, and another case, *Worcester* v. *Georgia*, would redefine the status of U.S. tribes and continue to affect Indian policy for at least another century.

Finders Keepers
By the time the Cherokee brought their plea to the Supreme Court, the justices had already ruled on an important case involving Indian tribes. In 1823 the Court ruled that the federal government, not Indian tribes, controlled ownership of land occupied by the tribes and had

the sole right to sell it. The unanimous decision, in the case of *Johnson & Graham's Lessee* v. *M'Intosh*, would set the course for all future dealings involving Indian land.

The case involved opposing claims by the heirs of a land company and a private landowner. Both sides claimed title to lands originally occupied by Indian tribes in territory that eventually became the state of Illinois. In 1773 the Illinois and Wabash land companies (later consolidated as the United Illinois and Wabash Land Companies) bought a large parcel of land from the Illinois tribe. The companies purchased a second large parcel in 1775 from the Piankeshaw Indians. Both purchases were made before the colonies became the United States. Heirs of the land company, Joshua Johnson and Thomas Jennings Graham, claimed title to the property. William McIntosh also claimed the property, saying that he owned approximately 11,560 acres in the same spot. He bought the land from the federal government in 1818.

The Supreme Court ruled that the land belonged to McIntosh. The opinion, written by Chief Justice John Marshall, decreed that the Indian tribes did not own the land and therefore could not sell it to the land companies. Ownership of the land had gone to the English crown when British agents "discovered" the territory, according to the Court. Once the colonists defeated the British in the American Revolution, the land passed to the U.S. government.

Chief Justice Marshall based his opinion on the Doctrine of Discovery, the theory that adventurers could claim ownership of undeveloped land merely by discovering it. The concept was used by all the European nations that set up colonies around the globe. Under the doctrine, natives held no power and no rights to ownership of the lands they occupied. The Europeans, and later the Americans, believed they had a duty to bring Christianity to the "uncivilized" people living in the wilderness. As the "discovering" nation, the invaders claimed control over the wild territory. Europeans and Americans introduced farming and manufacturing to the area as well as Christianity.

Often those who lived on lands taken over by other nations eventually blended in with the conquerors, Marshall noted. "The new and old members of the society mingle with each other; the distinction between them is gradually lost, and they make one people," he wrote. Once the two peoples united, Marshall wrote, public opinion and "wise policy" demanded that all be treated equally and that the conquered retain their property rights. But in his opinion, the Indians did not "blend" with the European settlers. The Indians, he contended, were "fierce savages, whose occupation was war, and whose subsistence was drawn chiefly from the forest." If the Indians had retained property rights, Marshall continued, then the Europeans would have had to abandon the country and it would have been left as a wilderness. They chose instead to subjugate the Indians and take over the land. The European king then awarded the land to those loyal to the crown.

European, and then American, control over Indian land had been well established for many years, Marshall said. Since that was the case, he noted, the system of ownership "becomes the law of the land, and cannot be questioned." Marshall accepted the system as "the actual condition" under which the ownership of land in America was determined. He concluded that Indians had a right to possess the land they now occupied, but they could not sell it. The chief justice declined to comment on whether the system was just or fair to the Indians.

Cherokee Nation v. Georgia

Marshall relied heavily on the Doctrine of Discovery in his decision in *Cherokee Nation* v. *Georgia*, which was issued in 1831. Noting the "universal recognition" of the doctrine's principles, Marshall ruled that the Indian tribes were not independent nations with sovereignty over their lands, but "domestic dependent nations" of the U.S. government. As such, the tribes had no right to sue a state. "Their relation to the United States resembles that of a ward to his guardian," the chief justice wrote. He concluded that Indian tribes were not true foreign nations apart from the United States:

> They look to our government for protection; rely upon its kindness and its power; appeal to it for relief to their wants; and address the president as their great father. They and their country are considered by foreign nations, as well as by ourselves, as being so completely under the sovereignty and dominion of the United States, that any attempt to acquire their lands, or to form a political connexion with them, would be considered by all as an invasion of our territory, and an act of hostility.

While acknowledging that the Indians had "an unquestionable, and heretofore, unquestioned right to the lands they occupy," Marshall nevertheless rejected the Cherokee plea that the Court protect their territory from Georgia's grasp. The Court, he said, could not issue such an order without interfering with the state's right to regulate itself. Fulfilling the tribe's request, Marshall noted, "requires us to control the legislature of Georgia." According to the decision, the federal government, not the courts, had sole jurisdiction over the tribes.

Two concurring justices, Baldwin and Johnson, wrote opinions even less supportive of tribal rights. Both argued that the Indians had no claim to sovereignty at all and that Georgia controlled their lands.

Justice Smith Thompson disagreed with Marshall's

majority opinion and presented a strong defense of the tribe's sovereignty. In his dissent Thompson argued that the Cherokee were in fact an independent, foreign nation and should be granted all the rights of a sovereign body. The United States had always before treated the Cherokee as a sovereign nation, he noted.

> They have been admitted and treated as a people governed solely and exclusively by their own laws, usages, and customs within their own territory, claiming and exercising exclusive dominion over the same; yielding up by treaty, from time to time, portions of their land, but still claiming absolute sovereignty and self government over what remained unsold.

The discovery doctrine should not apply to the tribes, Thompson contended, because they had never been conquered as a nation and forced to become subjects of the conqueror. Wars between the United States and Britain were settled by treaties, with neither side losing its status as a self-governing entity. The same pattern applied to wars between the tribes and the United States, which had always been settled by treaties that recognized the tribes as separate nations. Georgia was attempting to abolish the Cherokee government and "entirely [subvert] their national character," Thompson said. He argued that some of the state's laws were "so directly at variance with these [Indian] treaties and the laws of the United States touching the rights of property," that it was up to the Court to grant relief to the Cherokee. Justice Joseph Story concurred with the dissent.

Marshall's majority decision further encouraged Georgia and other states to encroach on Indian lands and ignore treaties with various tribes.

A COPY OF THE FIRST EDITION OF THE *Cherokee Phoenix*, PUBLISHED ON FEBRUARY 21, 1828. THE TRIBE'S NEWSPAPER WAS PRINTED IN BOTH ENGLISH AND CHEROKEE.

Another Try for Justice

Disappointed by the decision but undeterred, the Cherokee brought another case to the Court in 1832. This case involved Samuel Worcester, a minister who had lived among the Cherokee for many years. Given the name "The Messenger" by the tribe, Worcester was a close friend of Buck Oowatie, a Cherokee leader also known as Elias Boudinot. At Boudinot's request, Worcester helped set up the tribe's newspaper, the *Cherokee Phoenix*, in 1828. Funds from supporters of Worcester's missionary work paid expenses for the newspaper's office and for the printing press and type.

As pressure increased to uproot the tribe from Georgia, Worcester worked with tribal leaders to stop the removal. The American Board of Commissioners for Foreign Missions, a congregational group that supported Worcester's missionary work, helped finance the court efforts. After the ruling against the Cherokee in *Cherokee Nation* v. *Georgia*, the tribe needed another case to present to the Court. Wirt and Sergeant agreed to represent Worcester, who had been arrested for not obtaining a permit to work on tribal land. The minister came to the attention of state officials after he and eleven other white men signed a resolution at New Echota protesting the state law requiring such permits. Worcester faced charges of committing a "high misdemeanour," punishable by four years in jail.

In the lower court Wirt argued that the state's actions violated the sovereignty of the Cherokee Nation. Georgia had no authority to arrest Worcester for actions that occurred on Indian lands, he said. The lower court rejected the arguments and bound Worcester over for trial by jury. At the arraignment Worcester pled not guilty. After a short trial the jury found him and his fellow defendants guilty. The judge sentenced Worcester to four years of hard labor in the state penitentiary. Worcester appealed his conviction, and the case quickly made its way to the U.S. Supreme Court.

CENTRAL GOVERNMENT V. CONFEDERATION OF STATES

In addition to tribal rights, the *Worcester* case addressed an issue that played a central role in Marshall's career: states' rights versus the power of the federal government. Marshall had long fought for a strong national government during a time when individual states wanted to take control. In 1819, at the height of his power as chief justice, Marshall fought back efforts by the states to destroy the federal government's banking system. His decision in the case, *McCulloch* v. *Maryland*, has been described as a turning point in the history of the nation. It established the supremacy of the federal government over the states and gave Congress the power to overrule individual states' actions.

The *Worcester* case, which came near the end of Marshall's career, also involved a battle between the federal government and the states. As in *McCulloch*, an individual state (Georgia) took an action that interfered with federal matters (an Indian treaty). But there were a number of differences between the two cases. In *McCulloch*, President James Madison supported the bank's position against Maryland. In the *Worcester* case, however, President Andrew Jackson joined forces with Georgia against the tribe (and the federal treaty).

By 1832, when *Worcester* came before the Court, Marshall was nearing the end of an incredible term of office. In the early years, justices lived together at boardinghouses during the Court's term. Marshall won many justices over to his point of view during the casual conversation around the dinner table. Most decisions

CHIEF JUSTICE
JOHN MARSHALL

John Marshall is considered the greatest of the U.S. Supreme Court's chief justices. Even among the celebrated men who came before the Court as advocates during his long tenure, Chief Justice John Marshall dominated the proceedings. Called the "single most important figure on constitutional law," the Supreme Court's fourth chief justice was appointed to the post by President John Adams in 1801. He served the Court for thirty-four years, during which he wrote 519 opinions and oversaw more than 1,000 cases. From all accounts, his forceful personality—coupled with a superior intellect and high moral character—made him one of the most influential leaders of his time. He drew on his vast knowledge of the law and his exceptional powers of persuasion to sway associate justices to his point of view.

The oldest of fifteen children, Marshall was born in 1755 and grew up in the Blue Ridge foothills of Virginia. His father, a friend of George Washington, worked as a surveyor. His mother was a distant relative of Thomas Jefferson. The family, like those of other farmers in the region, owned slaves. He fought in the Revolutionary War, served in the Virginia House of Delegates, and practiced law in Richmond. After a short stint as Virginia's representative in Congress, he accepted President Adams's offer to serve as secretary of state. Shortly afterward, the president appointed him as chief justice. He held the position longer than any other chief justice in American history.

Marshall was an unpretentious, affectionate man, with an engaging personality that attracted people to him.

He liked to walk and read, play chess, and compete in an early game of horseshoes known as quoits, but he particularly enjoyed sociable gatherings with friends, who were drawn to his charm and sweet nature. Tall and thin, he paid little attention to his attire and often wore rumpled clothes that did not match—perhaps a remnant of his rustic upbringing. If his clothes were sometimes shabby, his intellect was not. His analytic mind enabled him to translate complex principles and theories into clear language that everyone could understand.

The Supreme Court's first chief justice, John Jay, resigned in despair that the Court would ever succeed in its mission. John Rutledge, the second chief justice, was forced to step down after only four months as acting chief when the Senate rejected President George Washington's nomination of him amid rumors that he suffered from mental illness. Oliver Ellsworth, the third man to serve as chief justice, had led the Senate committee that drafted the Judiciary Act of 1789 establishing the federal judiciary. He, however, contributed little of note in his nearly four years on the Court. When he resigned to negotiate a treaty with France, President John Adams asked Jay to step into the position again, but the disillusioned Jay declined. The Supreme Court, Jay said, operated "under a system so defective" that it would never be able to "obtain the energy, weight, and dignity which were essential" to supporting the national government or gaining the confidence and respect of the public. The president then handed the job of rebuilding the Court's prestige to John Marshall, who had previously turned down an offer to serve as an associate justice.

The decisions of the Marshall Court gave form to the new government, empowered Congress, and intervened in the power struggle between the states and the federal

JOHN MARSHALL WAS CHIEF JUSTICE OF THE UNITED STATES WHEN THE SUPREME COURT HEARD THE *WORCESTER* V. *GEORGIA* CASE.

government. An ardent Federalist who had lobbied for passage of the Constitution, Marshall molded the Court into an equal partner with the other branches of government. Under his guidance the Supreme Court used its power to overturn laws that—in the judgment of the Court—violated the Constitution. This power of judicial review, sanctioned by the 1803 case of *Marbury* v. *Madison*, became established doctrine. The ruling in the case authorized the Court to decide which laws were unconstitutional and put the Court on equal footing with the other two branches of government.

were unanimous, and justices rarely filed dissents even when they voted against the majority.

With Jackson's presidency, a new breed of associate justices came to the bench. They stayed at private homes and did not participate in the easy camaraderie of the past. Several supported states' claims over the federal government. As Marshall's influence waned, unanimous decisions became less common, and more justices issued opposing opinions on cases.

The national mood was changing as well. In the glory days after the American Revolution, people had been drawn together by a shared mission to form a new nation. Leaders such as George Washington, Alexander Hamilton, James Madison, and John Jay had helped convince Americans to band together under a strong federal government. Those days had passed. By the 1830s states were pushing for power with growing resolve. Their demands for control revolved around the issue of slavery. Southern and border states feared that a strong central government would ultimately abolish slavery. They clamored for states' rights to protect their ability to keep slaves within their borders. Eventually, of course, the states' battles would erupt into a civil war that would rip the nation apart.

FIVE
DECISION AND DEFIANCE

CONGRESS SET UP THE SUPREME COURT to rule on controversial issues. Chief Justice John Marshall knew the dangers of getting involved in a dispute that pitted the Court against the states and the president. But he saw no alternative. It was the Court's role to settle such matters. "This duty, however unpleasant, cannot be avoided," Marshall noted. "We must examine the defence set up in this plea."

Worcester v. *Georgia* certainly promised to be a controversial case. On the day of opening arguments, February 20, 1832, the U.S. House of Representatives adjourned because so many of its members attended the Court hearing. John Sergeant opened the arguments for Worcester and Elizur Butler, another missionary also involved in the case. Laying the groundwork with precision, Sergeant presented an argument that the *New York Daily Advertiser* described as "equally creditable to the soundness of his head and the goodness of his heart."

Wirt, who as attorney general had appeared before the Court many times and had argued in some of the nation's most important Supreme Court cases, followed with a lengthy and ardent speech to the six justices. Wirt's arguments did not end until after 3:00 p.m., when the fatigued lawyer asked for an adjournment. He was a handsome man with clear blue eyes and sandy hair, and often wore a

83

JOHN SERGEANT, A LAWYER AND POLITICIAN, SERVED AS COCOUNSEL WITH
WILLIAM WIRT REPRESENTING THE CHEROKEE NATION IN *WORCESTER* V.
GEORGIA. SERGEANT RAN UNSUCCESSFULLY FOR VICE PRESIDENT IN 1832 AND
SERVED SEVERAL TERMS IN CONGRESS.

swallowtail coat—a popular suit coat style of the time—and fashionable vest, tie, and breeches for his court appearances. Wirt's voice was his most effective tool. Musical and "hauntingly melodious," it captured the attention of his audience, according to historian John B. Boles.

Wirt and Sergeant concentrated on one argument: that Georgia's law under which Worcester had been arrested was unconstitutional. In making their case, Worcester's lawyers cited a number of treaties that had been approved by the Cherokee and ratified by the U.S. Senate. All of the pacts acknowledged the sovereignty of the Cherokee Nation and the Cherokee's right "to govern themselves, and all persons who have settled within their territory, free from any right of legislative interference by the . . . states."

According to the terms of the treaties, the federal government had guaranteed the land occupied by the Cherokee east of the Mississippi River to the tribe, the lawyers contended. No one was permitted to enter the territory without a passport or permission from the Cherokee. The tribe had allowed Worcester to live among them.

The lawyers argued that Georgia had no legal power to charge or prosecute Worcester and the other missionaries for actions that occurred within Cherokee territory. Furthermore, they said, the state had no authority to prevent white people from living in Cherokee lands or to order a guard to protect gold mines there. Georgia's laws requiring such actions were "unconstitutional, void, and of no effect," according to their argument. In addition to interfering with valid contracts between the Cherokee and the United States, such laws also illegally hindered trade with the Indians.

The *Cherokee Phoenix* reported that Wirt closed his remarks with such emotion that his words brought tears to John Marshall's eyes.

With assurances from President Jackson that he

RENOWNED LAWYER WILLIAM WIRT, A FORMER U.S. ATTORNEY GENERAL, REPRESENTED THE CHEROKEE NATION BEFORE THE U.S. SUPREME COURT.

would support the state's actions, Georgia did not even bother to send a representative to the Court hearing. As a result, the justices heard only Wirt's and Sergeant's arguments. As astute observers of their time, however, the justices were well aware of the political situation. They had heard the arguments on both sides of the issue and knew its importance.

The outcome would affect far more than the rights of two missionaries. As Chief Justice Marshall noted later in his opinion, the case involved matters "of the deepest interest." In reaching its decision, the Court would consider the claims of several entities: the powers of a state to pass laws, the power of the constitution and the federal government and their control over state actions, the rights of American Indians, and a citizen's personal liberty.

A DISTINCT COMMUNITY

Just twelve days later, on March 3, 1832, Chief Justice John Marshall delivered the Supreme Court's 5 to 1 decision in favor of Samuel Worcester and missionary Elizur Butler. The opinion did not, however, confirm the complete sovereignty of the Cherokee Nation. Rather, it put the power in the hands of the United States and followed Marshall's earlier decisions that favored a strong national government over individual states' rights.

While maintaining Marshall's earlier ruling in *Cherokee Nation* v. *Georgia* that tribes were domestic dependent nations, the decision did not totally abandon the rights of the Indians. The chief justice noted that "a weaker power does not surrender its independence—its right to self government, by associating with a stronger [power]." As a "distinct community, occupying its own territory, with boundaries accurately described," the Cherokee did not fall under the jurisdiction of Georgia, and the state had no power to enforce its laws on the tribe,

THROUGH THE COURT SYSTEM

First Stop: State Court

Almost all cases (about 95 percent) start in state courts. These courts go by various names, depending on the state in which they operate, such as circuit, district, municipal, county, or superior. The case is tried and decided by a judge, a panel of judges, or a jury.

The side that loses can then appeal to the next level.

First Stop: Federal Court

U.S. DISTRICT COURT—About 5 percent of cases begin their journey in federal court. Most of these cases concern federal laws, the U.S. Constitution, or disputes that involve two or more states. They are heard in one of the ninety-four U.S. district courts in the nation.

U.S. COURT OF INTERNATIONAL TRADE—Federal court cases involving international trade appear in the U.S. Court of International Trade.

U.S. COURT OF FEDERAL CLAIMS—The U.S. Court of Federal Claims hears federal cases against the U.S. government that involve more than $10,000, Indian tribes, and some disputes with government contractors. The loser in federal court can appeal to the next level.

Appeals: State Cases

Forty states have appeals courts that hear cases from the state courts. In states without an appeals court, the case goes directly to the state supreme court.

Appeals: Federal Cases

U.S. FEDERAL APPEALS COURTS—There are thirteen federal appellate courts: twelve U.S. circuit courts that handle cases appealed from the U.S. district courts and one U.S. Court of Appeals that decides cases appealed from the U.S. Court of International Trade and the U.S. Court of Federal Claims.

Each district court and every state and territory are assigned to one of the twelve circuits. Appeals in a few state cases—those that deal with rights guaranteed by the U.S. Constitution—are also heard in the circuit courts. Among the cases heard in the U.S. Court of Appeals are those involving patents and minor claims against the federal government.

Further Appeals: State Supreme Court
Cases appealed from state appeals courts go to the highest courts in the state—usually called the supreme court. In New York, however, the state's highest court is called the court of appeals. Most state cases do not go beyond this point.

Final Appeals: U.S. Supreme Court
The U.S. Supreme Court is the highest court in the country. Its decision on a case is the final word. The Court decides issues that can affect every person in the nation. It has decided cases on slavery, abortion, school segregation, and many other important issues.

The Court selects the cases it will hear—now around seventy-five each year. Four of the nine justices must vote to consider a case in order for it to be heard. Almost all cases have been appealed from the lower courts (either state or federal).

Most people seeking a decision from the Court submit a petition for *certiorari*. This means that the case will be moved from a lower court to a higher court for review. The Court receives more than nine thousand of these requests annually. The petition outlines the case and gives reasons why the Court should review it.

In rare cases, for example *New York Times* v. *United*

States (1971), an issue must be decided immediately. When such a case is of national importance, the Court allows it to bypass the usual lower court system and hears the case directly.

To win a spot on the Court's docket, a case must fall within one of the following categories:

- Disputes between states and the federal government or between two or more states.

- Cases involving ambassadors, consuls, and foreign ministers.

- Appeals from state courts that have ruled on a federal question.

- Appeals from federal appeals courts in cases in which appellate courts have issued conflicting decisions (about two-thirds of all requests fall into this category).

the Court observed. The ruling reversed the lower court's conviction of Samuel Worcester and Elizur Butler and ordered them set free. More importantly it eliminated state control over the tribes. Under the ruling, however, Congress continued to have control over Indian affairs.

In a surprising switch, Marshall's opinion followed the same arguments posed by Justice Smith Thompson in his dissent in the *Cherokee Nation* case. In *Worcester*, the chief justice ruled:

> The Cherokee nation, then, is a distinct community occupying its own territory, with boundaries accurately described, in which the laws of Georgia can have no force, and which the citizens of Georgia have no right to enter, but with the assent of the Cherokees themselves, or in conformity with treaties, and with the acts of Congress.

Marshall based his opinion on the treaties between the Cherokee and the U.S. government that guaranteed the tribe's status as a separate nation. The Constitution gave the federal government the power to execute the treaties, according to the chief justice. Those treaties, he said, remained in "full force," and had to be considered as "the supreme laws of the land."

Furthermore, Marshall said, the treaties threw a shield over the Cherokee, guaranteeing them "their rights of occupancy, of self-government, and the full enjoyment of those blessings which might be attained." By illegally forcing its laws on the tribe, Georgia had "broken in pieces" the shield protecting the tribe. Since states had jurisdiction only over people within their own territory, the Georgia state legislature had no authority to pass the Cherokee laws in an attempt to rule the tribe.

The chief justice noted that he had no comment on

whether the state laws were just or unjust. The Court's only concern, he said, was that Georgia had no right to enforce its laws on the Cherokee Nation. "We can look only to the law, which defines our power, and marks out the path of our duty," the opinion stated.

In the *Johnson* v. *M'Intosh* and the *Cherokee Nation* cases, Marshall had relied on, if not wholeheartedly endorsed, the concept that those who discovered a land took over possession from the native population. But in the *Worcester* decision, Marshall clearly questioned the so-called discovery doctrine and its effects. Did the early European settlers have the right to claim land that had belonged to Indians for centuries? Did farmers and manufacturers have a higher claim on lands occupied by hunters and fishermen?

Marshall concluded:

> It is difficult to comprehend the proposition, that the inhabitants of either quarter of the globe could have rightful original claims of dominion over the inhabitants of the other, or over the lands they occupied; or that the discovery of either by the other should give the discoverer rights in the country discovered, which annulled the preexisting rights of its ancient possessors.

According to Justice Hugo Black, it was one of Marshall's most eloquent and courageous decisions.

Justice William Johnson, who was absent from the Court, did not vote on the case. Presumably he would have joined Henry Baldwin in dissenting, given his views in the *Cherokee Nation* case. Baldwin, however, objected only on technical grounds and did not issue an opinion. Justices Joseph Story, Gabriel Duval, and Smith Thompson joined the majority opinion. Justice John McLean filed a concurring opinion, in which he dismissed the charges against the missionaries but suggested that the tribes might be better off if they moved west.

DEFYING THE COURT

The Cherokee rejoiced when they heard Marshall's words. They assumed that the decision meant they would be allowed to remain on their ancestral land. Jackson, however, was determined to move all the Indians out of the East, even the most "civilized" of tribes. When he learned of the Court ruling, Jackson is said to have replied, "John Marshall has rendered his decision, now let him enforce it."

Led by Chief John Ross, the tribe had conducted a tireless lobbying campaign to win support for their cause in Washington, D.C. Ross visited the capital countless times, enlisting the aid of influential people in Congress and elsewhere. Among those pledging support were Senator Henry Clay of Kentucky; Colonel David Crockett, who had fought with Jackson and Ross against the Creek in the War of 1812; Senator Daniel Webster; and U.S. Representative Edward Everett. The vote on the Indian Removal Act had been razor thin, indicating broad support among legislators for the Indians' cause. When it became apparent that Jackson intended to go ahead with his plan regardless of the Supreme Court order, however, there was no major outcry from the citizens at large. At the polls the following November voters gave Jackson a wide margin of victory in his bid for reelection.

With no public mandate in support of the Cherokee and with Jackson in the White House, the tribe's former supporters in Congress accepted that the removal was inevitable and virtually withdrew from the battle. Only the Cherokee, a few of their supporters, and a number of other tribes struggled on.

CHEROKEE LEADER JOHN ROSS, PICTURED IN 1841.

During the Battle at Horseshoe Bend, a Cherokee named Junaluska killed a Creek warrior about to slay Jackson. In desperation, Ross sent the man to plead with Jackson to allow the tribe to stay in their homes. According to a soldier who had befriended the Cherokee on the trek west, the president barely acknowledged the man to whom he owed his life. "Jackson's manner was cold and indifferent toward the rugged son of the forest who had saved his life. He met Junaluska, heard his plea but curtly said, 'Sir, your audience is ended. There is nothing I can do for you.'" Junaluska later regretted his actions because they allowed Jackson to live and go on to become president.

Missionaries Worcester and Butler remained in the state prison until January 1833. Wilson Lumpkin, the congressman who had spoken so forcefully for the Indian Removal Act, became governor of Georgia in 1831. He released the men after they agreed to give up the fight and end any further appeals. The American Board of Commissioners for Foreign Missions—Worcester's backer—believed the campaign to stop the removal of the Cherokee was fruitless and advised the missionaries to abandon the case. Worcester went to Oklahoma in 1835 and continued his missionary work with the tribe after the Cherokee arrived in Indian Territory three years later.

Assured that Jackson would not interfere, the Georgians set up a lottery in 1833 to dole out the Cherokee land. Prosperous Cherokee farmers were forced to give up their plantations, and residents their homes. When lottery winners claimed the tribe's government buildings in New Echota, the tribe established a new capital in Tennessee.

TREATY OF NEW ECHOTA

A faction of the Cherokee, led by Major Ridge, his son John, and his nephew Elias Boudinot, believed the situation was hopeless. They feared the entire Cherokee Nation would be destroyed if the tribe did not give up its lands and move west. On December 29, 1835, they and others signed the Treaty of New Echota, ceding 4.5 million acres of Cherokee land in Georgia, 1.6 million acres in Alabama, almost a million acres in Tennessee, and more than 700,000 acres in North Carolina. In exchange the tribe received 7 million acres of land in Indian Territory in the West and $5 million, which the federal government retained for the tribe's use.

After the signing, Jackson ordered his agent, John F. Schermerhorn, to arrange a conference with the tribe to poll members on their views regarding the treaty. Of the more than 16,000 tribe members, only a handful attended the meeting. Of those voting, 79 approved the treaty; seven voted against it. Schermerhorn claimed that all those not at the meeting favored the treaty, a blatant distortion of the truth. Tribe members later executed Boudinot, Major Ridge, and John Ridge for their role in the affair.

A report filed by Major William M. Davis, the federal agent sent to record tribe members in preparation for the removal, contradicted Schermerhorn's claims. "That paper called a treaty is no treaty at all because [it was] not sanctioned by the great body of Cherokee, and made without their participation or assent," Davis wrote in a March 5, 1836, letter to the secretary of war. He said that if the Cherokee people were given a chance to vote on the treaty, "it would be instantly rejected by nine-tenths of them and I believe by nineteen-twentieths of them." Sixteen thousand Cherokee signed a document circulated by Ross asserting they had never approved the treaty.

Nevertheless, the House tabled the Cherokee request to stop the enforced move, and on May 23, 1836, the Senate ratified the Treaty of New Echota by one vote. The tribe was given two years to move west; after that, the Cherokee would be forced from their tribal lands.

In a last-ditch effort to spare the tribe, John Ross made a personal plea to the members of Congress in a letter written September 28, 1836. It read in part:

> Our hearts are sickened. . . . We are deprived of membership in the human family! We have neither land nor home nor resting place that can be called our own. . . . In truth our cause is your own; it is the cause of liberty and justice; it is based on your own principles which we have learned from yourselves; for we have gloried to count your Washington and your Jefferson our great teachers. . . . Before your august assembly we present ourselves, in the attitude of deprecation and of entreaty. On your kindness, on your humanity, on your compassion, on your benevolence, we rest our hopes. To you we address our reiterated prayers. Spare our people! Spare the wreck of our prosperity!

As eloquent as Ross's words were, they had no effect against the power of the federal will.

Meanwhile other southern tribes were making the trek to Jackson's promised utopia in the West. The reality—at least for members of the various tribes—turned out to be nothing like Jackson's vision. On March 24, 1832, the Creek of Alabama and Georgia signed a treaty that set the stage for their trek west. Though the treaty specified that individual members of the tribe "shall be free to go or stay," crooked land deals left the members destitute and forced them to move west. A U.S. marshal who had observed the land fiasco, commented in disgust:

> I have never seen corruption carried on to such proportions in all my life. A number of the land

purchasers think it rather an honor than a dishonor to defraud the Indian out of his land.

During the winter of 1836 to 1837 almost 15,000 Creek began the thousand-mile journey west. Bent in defeat and burdened by the weight of their meager possessions, they trudged their way through the Oklahoma snow, some walking with bare feet across the frozen ground. Abandoned belongings littered the path. Government troops accompanying the sad caravan pledged to retrieve the treasures later and return them to tribe members, but the promise was never kept. Vultures overhead marked where the dead lay.

SIX
A TRAIL OF TEARS

SOON AFTER THE SENATE VOTE on the Treaty of New Echota, the Cherokee in the Ridge faction moved to Indian Territory. The rest of the tribe remained in their eastern homes. As the deadline neared, Georgia officials threatened to call in the state militia to force the tribe across the Mississippi River if the federal government failed to take action. By then Martin Van Buren, a New Yorker who had served as Jackson's vice president, had assumed the presidency. Carrying out Jackson's Indian policies, he ordered the army to forcibly remove the Cherokee from Georgia. On the appointed day, May 23, 1838, General Winfield Scott and seven thousand federal troops marched into Cherokee towns to begin the removal.

Bargain hunters crowded the streets of Cherokee towns, eager to get a deal on household goods, buildings, and other property. Desperate to sell their possessions before the move, the Cherokee agreed to prices far below true value. One Cherokee man told of an auction held at his house in those last frantic days before the trek west. His family's china, edged in blue, sold for twenty-five cents a plate. He never received any money from the auction, which likely ended up in the pockets of the auctioneer.

Officials promised the Cherokee that their belongings would be delivered to them once they reached their destination. But even before the travelers were out of sight,

MEMBERS OF AN AMERICAN INDIAN FAMILY CARRY THEIR POSSESSIONS IN PACKS ON THE BACKS OF THEIR DOGS. DURING FORCED MIGRATIONS TO THE WEST, THOUSANDS OF MEN, WOMEN, AND CHILDREN DIED.

thugs broke windows, smashed doors, and looted homes of anything of value. "Many an Indian turning for a farewell look saw his house going up in flames," historian Walter Hart Blumenthal wrote.

Marshals herded the Cherokee into camps under armed guard, where they waited for the long trek to begin. Almost 18,000 Cherokee men, women, and children "were dragged from their homes, and driven at the bayonet point into the stockades," wrote John G. Burnett, one of the soldiers who accompanied the Cherokee on their long trek west. Soldiers kept the line moving, prodding with bayonets those who walked too slowly. One man whose spouse had been pricked by a bayonet lashed out against the offending soldier and was handcuffed and lashed one hundred times with a whip. The sick and dying were carried into the camps on stretchers. Many died that summer, crammed into the hot camps without clean water or adequate waste treatment.

The Cherokee National Council issued one last resolution on August 1, 1838, from the Aquohee Camp in Rattlesnake Springs, Tennessee, where the tribe was imprisoned until the removal began. The edict, defiant and unbending, read in part:

> Whereas: the title of the Cherokee people to their lands is the most ancient, pure, and absolute, known to man; its date is beyond the reach of human record; its validity confirmed and illustrated by possession and enjoyment, antecedent to all pretense of claim by any other portion of the human race; and

> Whereas: the free consent of the Cherokee people is indispensable to a valid transfer of the Cherokee title; and

Whereas: the said Cherokee people have, neither by themselves nor their representatives, given such consent;

It follows, that the original title and ownership of said lands still rest in the Cherokee Nation, unimpaired and absolute;

Resolved, therefore, . . . that the whole Cherokee territory, as described in the first article of the treaty of 1819 between the United States and the Cherokee Nation, and, also, in the constitution of the Cherokee Nation, still remains the rightful and undoubted property of the said Cherokee Nation; . . . and

Whereas: the Cherokee people have existed as a distinct national community, in the possession and exercise of the appropriate and essential attributes of sovereignty, for a period extending into antiquity beyond the dates and records and memory of man; and

Whereas: these attributes, with the rights and franchises which they involve, have never been relinquished by the Cherokee people, but are now in full force and virtue; and

Whereas: the natural, political, and moral relations subsisting among the citizens of the Cherokee Nation, toward each other and towards the body politic, cannot, in reason and justice, be dissolved by the expulsion of the nation from its own territory by the power of the United States Government;

CHEROKEE REMOVAL ROUTES

National Historic Trail •••• Land Route ▬ Water Route ▬ Other Major Routes

THIS MAP SHOWS FOUR OF THE ROUTES FOLLOWED BY THE CHEROKEE DURING THEIR FORCED MIGRATION TO OKLAHOMA.

Resolved, therefore, . . . that the inherent sovereignty of the Cherokee Nation, together with the constitution, laws, and usages, of the same, are, and, by the authority aforesaid, hereby declared to be in full force and virtue, and shall continue so to be in perpetuity.

A TREK OF 1,200 MILES
Four hundred Cherokee escaped into the mountains. Their descendants, known as the Eastern Cherokee, remain in the region, living on a 60,000-acre reservation

in North Carolina. The others embarked on a forced march through rough terrain and wilderness. The first groups left shortly after the Cherokee National Council issued its edict. Like the Chickasaw, the Creek, and the Choctaw before them, the Cherokee suffered immeasurable sadness and pain along the Trail of Tears, the name they gave to the long path west.

Soldier Burnett continued his description of the expedition:

> In the chill of a drizzling rain on an October morning I saw them loaded like cattle or sheep into six hundred and forty-five wagons and started toward the west.
>
> One can never forget the sadness and solemnity of that morning. Chief John Ross led in prayer and when the bugle sounded and the wagons started rolling many of the children rose to their feet and waved their little hands good-by to their mountain homes, knowing they were leaving them forever. Many of these helpless people did not have blankets and many of them had been driven from home barefooted.

The Cherokee walked throughout the winter of 1838. On November 17 the temperature dropped below freezing, and sleet and snow fell on the trail. From that day until March 26, 1839, when the last of the tribe finally arrived at their destination, "the sufferings of the Cherokee were awful," according to Burnett. "The trail of the exiles was a trail of death. They had to sleep in the wagons and on the ground without fire. I have known as many as twenty-two of them to die in one night of pneumonia due to ill treatment, cold, and exposure."

Food left for the tribe by government agents rotted on the trail before they reached it. Some rode in wagons, others on horseback; many walked the entire journey on foot. Those too sick to continue were left behind on the trail. Wolves followed the tribe, digging up the graves of the dead. It took at least four months for each group to cover the 1,200 miles to the new lands. After months of horror, broken-spirited, sick, and starving, the last of the Cherokee straggled into Indian Territory. Four thousand people died during the ordeal.

In his December 1838 message to Congress, President Van Buren reported that the Indian Removal Act had "had the happiest effects. . . . The Cherokee have emigrated without any apparent reluctance."

removal of other tribes

Between 1830 and the mid–1840s almost all of the nation's 90,000 eastern American Indians were driven west across the Mississippi River. During just the eight years of Jackson's term in office, Congress approved about seventy treaties with eastern tribes. The army's efforts to move the Seminole west from Florida sparked a seven-year war that raged from 1835 to 1842. The tribe fought on after the death of their leader, but U.S. forces eventually seized about four thousand Seminole and marched them under guard to Indian Territory. A small band escaped to the Florida Everglades, where their descendants still live.

A few northern tribes remained in Maine and other sparsely populated areas. With the help of powerful Quakers, several groups of Iroquois managed to stay in New York. Some migrated to Canada. Most of the others, however, moved west. The Sauk (also called Sac) and Fox tribes of Wisconsin and Illinois made the trek across the Mississippi to lands in Iowa in the early 1830s. After a harsh winter in the new lands, the tribes returned to plant crops in their homelands to the east. Their return sparked the Black Hawk War, the last war waged by the tribes in the old Northwest Territory. Black Hawk, an eloquent chief, led the tribes in the bloody and ill-fated conflict that left five hundred Indians dead, many of them women and children. After their defeat, the tribes were forced to cede all their eastern lands and move to a reservation in Iowa.

LIFE IN THE WEST: ENEMY TRIBES AND WHITE HOMESTEADERS

For the new arrivals the West was far from the paradise officials had promised. The upheaval caused by the removal had shredded the fabric of the lives of the Cherokee. Loved ones were dead, tribes had separated, and families split into factions. Property and wealth had vanished. With little left from their past, the survivors of the march focused on setting up villages and learning how to live in the foreign land where they had been driven. They had to cope with poverty and a harsh climate. Despondent Cherokee succumbed to alcoholism and became easy marks for unscrupulous traders who sold whiskey and rum along the borders of Indian Territory.

The first year in the West was further complicated by the bitter divide between the tribe's two factions. Many of those who had resisted removal until the end believed those who had signed the Treaty of New Echota had sold out the tribe. In June 1839 an unidentified band of Cherokee ambushed and killed three of the signers—John Ridge, Major Ridge, and Elias Boudinot. The killings only increased the friction between the two sides. In addition, problems developed between the newcomers and a group of Cherokee who had voluntarily left Georgia in 1817 and settled in the West. These "Old Settlers" had migrated before the eastern tribe had set up its U.S.-based government. They operated under the old traditional system.

The Cherokee and other eastern tribes also faced the anger of the Plains Indians, who claimed the western lands as their own.

John Ross managed to hold the tribe together, and eventually the Cherokee united under the constitutional system established in the 1820s. The new nation set up schools and erected government buildings, printed a newspaper called the *Cherokee Advocate*, and prospered as farmers and cattle herders.

Land-hungry Americans soon followed the tribes across the Mississippi River. Part of the Cherokee tribe had moved to Kansas under an 1854 agreement, but after being forced to cede parcels of their land based on several new treaties, the Kansas Cherokee had to abandon the new territory altogether in 1868 and join the rest of the tribe in Oklahoma.

CIVIL War

When the Civil War erupted in 1861, Ross and others did their best to keep the tribe out of the conflict. When the Confederate Army gained control of the surrounding area, however, the Cherokee had little choice but to pledge support to the South. A treaty between the two powers pledged that the tribe would have a say in a Confederate government, that Cherokee representatives would serve in the rebels' congress, and that the tribe would have the right to tax traders in their territory. The war reopened the divisions in the tribe. Some Cherokee fought loyally for the South; others deserted or joined Union forces.

After being taken captive by the Union Army, John Ross met with President Abraham Lincoln to pledge the tribe's support. He rejected the Confederate pact, saying the tribe had been forced to sign it. Later the Cherokee rescinded the treaty and freed the slaves in their territory. But fighting between Cherokee on both sides continued until the war ended in 1865. The conflict left the Cherokee Nation decimated: one-third of the tribe was dead, buildings and crops were destroyed, and belongings were gone. In the aftermath of the war, Congress stripped a large parcel of their land from the tribe, justifying the action by charging that the Cherokee had sided with the Confederacy.

seven
A Tribe's Survival

In 1871 congress passed a thirty-page appropria-
tions bill that banned further treaties with the tribes.
Reflecting John Marshall's views in the *Cherokee Nation*
decision forty years before, the bill also decreed that
tribes would not be considered independent nations.
Though designed to end treaty abuses, the bill resulted in
the further division of tribal land by taking away the
Indians' status as tribes.

On February 8, 1887, Congress passed the General
Allotment Act, which ordered that all American Indian
land be divided among tribe members. Many supporters of
the bill believed that by holding title to their own lands,
individual Indians would have a better chance of blending
into the white population. These advocates hoped such
assimilation would ease tensions between the two cultures
and help Indians protect their lands and prosper. The bill,
however, had the opposite effect. Used to managing land as
a tribe, individual Indians had no experience or desire to
farm single plots of land. Many sold their tracts to whites
who surged into the area. As a result of the Allotment Act,
most of western Oklahoma was opened to white homesteaders. By the end of 1889 the western half of Indian Territory had become the Territory of Oklahoma.

The members of the relocated Five Civilized Tribes
retained their lands in eastern Oklahoma, occupying

MEMBERS OF THE CHEROKEE TRIBE HOLD A CEREMONY IN OKLAHOMA ON
MAY 16, 1951, AFTER RETRACING THE ROUTE FOLLOWED BY THEIR ANCESTORS
DURING THE TRAIL OF TEARS. *FROM LEFT,* ARSENE THOMPSON, TRIBAL MIN-
ISTER OF CHEROKEE COUNTY, OKLAHOMA; JOE LYNCH, OKLAHOMA JUDGE;
LEROY WASHINGTON; LEROY WAHNETA; AND VICE CHIEF MCKINLEY ROSE,
WHO MIXES SOIL FROM OKLAHOMA WITH THAT FROM THE GREAT SMOKY
MOUNTAINS IN NORTH CAROLINA AND TENNESSEE.

20 million acres. The five tribes united under their own government and in 1905 drew up a constitution for a proposed state to be called Sequoyah. At a convention in Muskogee, Oklahoma, on August 21, 1905, members of the various tribes considered whether to seek statehood themselves or to merge with Oklahoma when the territory became a state. Most full-blooded American Indians argued vehemently to set up Sequoyah as a separate state. Those of mixed blood, however, generally argued for the merger, and their forces eventually won.

When Oklahoma entered the Union in 1907, Congress doled out portions of the eastern section among the individual American Indians who lived there. The U.S. government sold the land left over to white settlers. Again thousands of prospective landowners gathered to claim what had once been tribal lands.

Separate Entities and Self-Determination

After centuries of trying to force tribes to sell off their land and ignoring their sovereignty, the U.S. government finally changed course. In 1934 Congress passed the Indian Reorganization Act, also known as the Wheeler-Howard Act, which stopped the division of tribal lands. It also recognized tribes as separate entities, but not as completely independent nations. Under the law, tribes once again were permitted to run their own affairs; set up their own governments; and negotiate with federal, state, and local bodies. The federal government, but not the states, continued to hold power over the tribes, however, as stipulated by John Marshall in the Supreme Court's *Worcester* decision a century before.

The Indian Claims Commission, which Congress established in 1946, gave tribes a chance to seek restitution from the United States for past land abuses. More than 170 tribes filed 370 complaints with the commission during the thirty-two years the commission operated. By the time it closed down, the commission had awarded a total of $818 million to tribes. Most of the money went to pay for land taken by treaties at prices far below the fair value.

The government shifted policy again in the 1950s when it focused on relocating American Indians to cities and ending the government's relationship with the tribes. By the end of 1956 almost ten thousand American Indians had left their reservations and worked in cities. The policy change was accompanied by a reduction in federal funds for social service programs and an end to government loans for American Indians to encourage them to leave the reservations. To cope with the overwhelming financial burdens the new policy caused, many of the tribes sold their holdings, and their members dispersed.

During the 1960s and 1970s young American Indian activists took over buildings, blocked roads, and held demonstrations to protest the government's treatment of the tribes. Their actions, including an armed confrontation with federal troops at Wounded Knee, South Dakota, in 1973, drew attention to their cause and renewed pride among American Indians in old tribal ways. Many non-Indian Americans expressed sympathy for the tribes' cause.

In 1975 Congress repealed the termination acts of the 1950s and in the next few years enacted a series of new laws, among them the Indian Self-Determination Act, the Indian Child Welfare Act, and the Indian Health Care Improvement Act. These laws reinstated federal aid and reestablished the relationship between the federal government and the tribes, but turned over responsibility for tribal affairs and government to the tribes. However, the management and administration of 55.7 million acres of tribal lands was assigned to the Bureau of Indian Affairs. The land continues to be held in trust for the tribes by the United States.

Subsequent court cases and acts of Congress have further defined the status of tribes and settled long-standing disputes over rights and lands. In response to a 1980 Maine Supreme Court case, Congress passed the Maine Indian Land Claims Settlement Act, which gave American Indians in Maine $81.5 million in trust fund money and timberland as payment for lands taken from them by the government during the last centuries. Another court settlement gave tribes in Washington State the right to 50 percent of the salmon caught each year in Puget Sound.

In 1992 Congress passed a bill that provided low-interest loans to American Indians, enabling them to buy their own homes. The loans, backed by the U.S. Department of Housing and Urban Development, also helped American Indians to renovate their homes. In 2007 Congress approved the Native American Home Ownership Opportunity Act, extending the loan program through 2012.

As citizens of the United States, the Cherokee and all American Indians can vote, own property, and live wherever they choose. Those who live on Cherokee land, however, are governed by the Cherokee Nation, federally recognized as the tribe's official government. The tribe operates under a new constitution, approved by the Cherokee people and enacted in 2006. For the most part, the tribe, the second largest in the nation, has retained the same democratic system as in John Ross's day: a representative legislature (now a single tribal council), a principal chief and a deputy chief elected by the people to four-year terms, and an independent judiciary.

Still surviving, too, is the essence of any nation's existence: the power to govern its own people. By law and treaty, the tribe has sovereignty over its people. In the

Members of Congress, tribal members, and others gather around as President George W. Bush signs the Native American Home Ownership Opportunity Act of 2007 on June 18, 2007. *From left,* Housing and Urban Development Secretary Alphonso Jackson; Seminole Nation Principal Chief Enoch Haney; Cherokee Nation Principal Chief Chad Corntassel Smith; Representative Dan Boren, D-Oklahoma; Chickasaw Nation Governor Bill Anoatubby; President Bush; Representative Tom Cole, R-Oklahoma; Choctaw Nation Assistant Chief Gary Batton; and Creek Nation Principal Chief A. D. Ellis.

words of Principal Chief Chad Smith, reporting to the tribe in the nation's 2006 annual report, "Sovereignty is the most precious possession held by our tribe. It is the foundation of our government and the glue that binds our people together."

racism or a threat to sovereignty?
A dispute over membership in the Cherokee Nation may well return the tribe to the U.S. Supreme Court with a case

that could affect the tribe's sovereignty. The conflict arose over whether the descendants of the slaves who traveled west with the Cherokee should be considered full-fledged members of the tribe. In the 1866 treaty signed by the Cherokee after the Civil War, the tribe's freed slaves became full members of the nation. A tribal decree issued in 1983, however, barred the black Cherokee, or Freedmen, from voting on tribal matters because they did not have "Cherokee blood." The tribe's supreme court overrode the decree in December 2006, ruling that denying the Freedmen the right to vote violated the Cherokee Constitution.

The controversy escalated in March 2007 when the nation voted to exclude the Freedmen from the tribe. About 25,000 of the tribe's 270,000 members are considered Freedmen. Tribal members qualify for a host of federal programs, including housing, medical care, and educational benefits, as well as a share in earnings from casinos and other enterprises owned and operated by the tribes.

Those who favor the vote believe that only blood relatives of Cherokee should be members. They say the issue is not one of race, but of tribal sovereignty. The tribe, they maintain, has a right to determine who qualifies as a citizen of the nation. They rely on a census of tribal members drawn up in 1906 called the Dawes Roll to determine blood lines. When the Dawes Roll was compiled, all those with mixed white and Cherokee ancestry went on the list; however, black Cherokee—even those who were half Cherokee—were put on a separate list.

The Freedmen argue that they have lived their entire lives as Cherokee and have always considered themselves members of the tribe. Their ancestors, they note, walked the Trail of Tears along with their Cherokee masters. Furthermore, many of the Freedmen claim Cherokee ancestors. Most of the white tribal members have less than one-quarter Cherokee blood. "There are Freedmen who can prove they have a full-blooded Cherokee grandfather who won't be members," Marilyn Vann, president of the Descendants of Freedmen of the Five Civilized Tribes told a *New York Times* reporter in March 2007. "And there are blond people who are 1/1000th Cherokee who are members."

Even proof of Cherokee blood by DNA testing may not resolve the issue. Those who oppose Freedmen membership in the tribe argue that Freedmen should have to meet the standards of other Cherokee, who traditionally trace their American Indian heritage back to a particular tribe member. DNA may indicate that Freedmen have a Cherokee ancestor, but it cannot name the specific person.

Freedmen supporters say such arguments smack of racism. Meanwhile, the Freedmen are pursuing the case in federal court. Members of Congress have threatened to withdraw federal benefits from tribes that bar black members. A court ruling could also override the tribe's sovereignty by ordering the black members' reinstatement.

The controversy has disturbed many in the tribe. "This is a sad chapter in Cherokee history," Taylor Keen, a member of the Cherokee tribal council and supporter of the Freedmen cause told a *New York Times* reporter in 2007. "But this is not my Cherokee Nation. My Cherokee Nation is one that honors all parts of her past."

Perhaps another U.S. Supreme Court ruling will decide the matter. And this time, if Justice Stephen Breyer's assessment is correct, the president will not defy the Court's decision.

NOTES

Introduction

p. 7, par. 2; p. 9, par. 3–4, Stephen Breyer, "Our Civic Commitment," Annual Meeting of the American Bar Association, Chicago, August 4, 2001, Supreme Court of the United States, http://www.supremecourtus.gov/publicinfo/speeches/sp_08-04-01.html

p. 8, par. 3, Randall Bennett Woods, *Quest for Identity: America Since 1945* (New York: Cambridge University Press, 2005), 90.

p. 8, par. 4, "The Southern Manifesto," *Congressional Record*, 84th Congress Second Session, 102, part 4 (March 12, 1956) (Washington, D.C.: Governmental Printing Office, 1956), 4459–4460.

Chapter 1

p. 13, par. 1, Thomas Jefferson, "Letter from Thomas Jefferson to the Deputies of the Cherokees of the upper and lower towns," January 9, 1809, American Memory, Library of Congress, http://memory.loc.gov/cgi-bin/query/P?mtj:2:./temp/~ammem_NhNQ::

p. 15, par. 3, "John Ross Chief of the Cherokee," Georgian Tribe of Eastern Cherokee, http://www.georgiatribeof easterncherokee.com/chiefjohnross.htm

p. 15, par. 4, "John Ross," About Georgia, http://ngeorgia.com/ang/John_Ross

p. 16, par. 1, Laurel M. Sheppard, "An Interview with

Mary Ross, First Native American Woman Engineer,"
Lash Publications, http://www.lashpublications.com/
maryross.htm

p. 18, par. 1, James W. Parins, "The Greatness of
Sequoyah," American Native Press Archives and
Sequoyah Research Center, http://anpa.ualr.edu/
digital_library/The%20Genius%20of%20Sequoyah.htm

p. 18, par. 2, Walter Hart Blumenthal, *American Indians
Dispossessed* (New York: Ayer Company Publishing,
1975), 76–77.

p. 18, par. 3, John J. Lalor, ed., "Cherokee Case,"
Cyclopaedia of Political Science (New York: Maynard,
Merrill, and Company, 1899).

p. 19, par. 1–2, "New Echota Historic Site," About North
Georgia, http://ngeorgia.com/ang/New_Echota_
Historic_Site

p. 20, par. 2, Herman J. Viola, *After Columbus: The Smithsonian Chronicle of the North American Indians* (New
York: Orion Books, 1990), 137.

p. 21, par. 1, Louis Filler and Allen Guttmann, eds., *The
Removal of the Cherokee Nation: Manifest Destiny or
National Dishonor* (Lexington, MA: D. C. Heath, 1962), 18.

Chapter 2

p. 25, par. 1, William Bradford, "Extracts from the History
of Plimoth Plantation," The Secretary of the Commonwealth by Order of the General Court, Boston, 1900,
http://www.mayflowerhistory.com/PrimarySources/
MourtsRelation.pdf

p. 25, par. 3, Black Hawk, *Autobiography of Ma-Ka-Tai-Me-
She-Kia-Kiak, or Black Hawk* (St. Louis: Press of Continental Printing Co., 1882; first edition, 1833). Project
Gutenberg Literary Archive Foundation,
http://www.gutenberg.org/catalog/world/readfile?fk_
files=9061&pageno=38

p. 30, par. 2, William Penn, "Address to the American
Indians," 1682, Quakers on Peace, The Religious
Society of Friends, http://www.quaker.org/fmw/
quakersonpeace.pdf

p. 31, par. 1, Hugh Barbour and J. William Frost, *The Quakers*
(Richmond, IN: Friends United Press, 1988), 75.

p. 32, par. 1, "Cherokee Chiefs in London, 1762," *New
York Times*, October 26, 1884, 11.

p. 33, par. 3–p. 34, par. 1, Walter Hart Blumenthal, *American Indians Dispossessed* (New York: Ayer Company
Publishing, 1975), 52.

p. 34, par. 2, Herman J. Viola, *After Columbus: The Smithsonian Chronicle of the North American Indians* (New
York: Orion Books, 1990), 110.

p. 35, par. 1, Michael Sims, "The Treaty of Sycamore
Shoals—A 'Dark and Bloody' Treaty," *The Great Cherokees*, The Chickamaugans Web site, http://www.angel
fire.com/tn2/inada/chickamauga/stolen_land.html

p. 35, par. 2, Chief Dragging Canoe, "Tsalagi (Cherokee)
Literature," cited in Indigenous Peoples' Literature
Index Page by Glenn Welker, http://www.indians.org/
welker/cherokee.htm

p. 36, par. 1, "Proclamation of Lord Dunmore against
Richard Henderson and his Abettors," March 21, 1775
(from the *Virginia Gazette* in the Library of Congress);
"Proclamation of Governor Martin of North Carolina
against Richard Henderson and his Confederates,"
February 10, 1775 (from Volume IX, Colonial Records
of North Carolina); Journal, Virginia House of Delegates, November 17, 1778.

p. 37, par. 3, Thomas Jefferson, "Letter to Edmund
Pendleton, Philadelphia, August 13, 1776," Avalon
Project at Yale Law School, http://www.yale.edu/
lawweb/avalon/jefflett/let8.htm

p. 37, par. 4, Jefferson, "Letter to Edmund Pendleton."

p. 41, par. 4, Alvin M. Josephy Jr., *500 Nations: An Illustrated History of North American Indians* (New York: Gramercy, 2002), 44.

p. 42, par. 2, Jerri-Jo Idarius, "The Iroquois Confederacy," *Sojourn Magazine*, winter 1998, http://www.lightparty.com/Spirituality/Iroquois.html

p. 43, par. 1–2, Wilcomb E. Washburn, "Indians and the American Revolution," http://www.american revolution.org/ind1.html

p. 43, par. 3, Viola, *After Columbus: The Smithsonian Chronicle of the North American Indians*, 118.

p. 43, par. 5–p. 44, par. 1, Northwest Ordinance, Article III, An Ordinance for the Government of the Territory of the United States Northwest of the River Ohio, July 13, 1787, "Historic Documents of the United States," America's Homepage. http://ahp.gatech.edu/nw_ordinance_1787.html

p. 44, par. 5–p. 45, par. 1, Derrick Z. Jackson, "The Face of Bush's America," *Boston Globe*, July 20, 2001, editorial.

p. 45, par. 2, Josephy, *500 Nations*, 278.

p. 46, par. 1, Blumenthal, *American Indians Dispossessed*, 27.

p. 46, par. 3, Henry Adams, *History of the United States of America During the Administrations of Thomas Jefferson* (New York: The Library of America, 1986), 343.

Chapter 3

p. 49, par. 2, Herman J. Viola, *After Columbus: The Smithsonian Chronicle of the North American Indians* (New York: Orion Books, 1990), 110.

p. 50, par. 3, "Thomas Jefferson: Answers to de Meusnier Questions, 1786," ME 17:74. "Thomas Jefferson on Politics & Government," University of Virginia Library, http://etext.virginia.edu/jefferson/quotations/jeff1300.htm

p. 53, par. 2, Henry Adams, *History of the United States of*

America During the Administrations of Thomas Jefferson (New York: The Library of America, 1986), 1197.

pp. 54–56, The Indian Removal Act of 1830, U.S. Government Document, http://www.ourdocuments.gov. Transcript: http://www.civics-online.org/library/formatted/texts/indian_act.html

p. 57, par. 1, Frank E. Smitha, "Canada and the United States, 1814 to 1846," MacroHistory: Prehistory to Yesterday, http://www.fsmitha.com/h3/h40-am.html, and U.S. Census, "Population, Housing Units, Area Measurements, and Density: 1790 to 1990," http://www.census.gov/population/censusdata/table-2.pdf

p. 57, par. 3, "Exchange of Lands with the Indians," No. 145, U.S. American State Papers, Senate, 14th Congress, 2nd Session Indian Affairs: vol. 2, 123. Presented to the Senate January 9, 1817.

p. 57, par. 4–p. 58, par. 1, Walter Hart Blumenthal, *American Indians Dispossessed* (New York: Arno Press, 1975), 22.

p. 58, par. 2, Library of Congress, Indian Affairs: vol. 2, Senate 18th Congress, 2nd session, 542, January 27, 1825.

p. 59, par. 3, "The Hermitage, Home of President Andrew Jackson," The Hermitage Web site, http://www.thehermitage.com/

p. 60, par. 1, "Andrew Jackson," Information Services Branch of the State Library of North Carolina, http://statelibrary.dcr.state.nc.us/nc/bio/public/jackson.htm

p. 61, par. 1, Richard B. Latner, "Andrew Jackson: Indian Removal," *Journal of American History*, 76:1, June 1989.

p. 62, par. 1, Andrew Jackson, 1829 State of the Union Address, December 8, 1828, "Historic Speeches," http://www.presidentialrhetoric.com

p. 62, par. 3, Rennard J. Strickland and William M. Strickland, "The Court and the Trail of Tears,"

Supreme Court Historical Society, http://www.supremecourthistory.org

p. 63, par. 2, (Lumpkin) Gales & Seaton's Register of Debates in Congress (Congressional Register), House of Representatives, 21st Congress, 1st Session, May 17, 1830, 1016–1026.

p. 63, par. 3, (Wilde) Gales & Seaton's Register of Debates in Congress (Congressional Register), House of Representatives, 21st Congress, 1st Session, May 19, 1830, 1080–1084.

p. 63, par. 4, (Lamar) Gales & Seaton's Register of Debates in Congress (Congressional Register), House of Representatives, 21st Congress, 1st Session, May 19, 1830, 1112–1120.

p. 63, par. 5–p. 64, par. 1, 2, (Storrs) Gales & Seaton's Register of Debates in Congress (Congressional Register), House of Representatives, 21st Congress, 1st Session, May 15, 1830, 994–1015.

p. 64, par. 3–p. 64, par. 1, (Evans) Gales & Seaton's Register of Debates in Congress (Congressional Register), House of Representatives, 21st Congress, 1st Session, May 18, 1830, 1037–1049.

p. 65, par. 2, Gales & Seaton's Register of Debates in Congress (Congressional Register), House of Representatives, 21st Congress, 1st Session, May 19, 1830, 674.

p. 65, par. 3, Gales & Seaton's Register of Debates in Congress (Congressional Register), House of Representatives, 21st Congress, 1st Session, May 15, 1830, 994–1148.

p. 66, par. 1, 2, Blumenthal, *American Indians Dispossessed*, 94, 101.

p. 66, par. 3; p. 68, par. 1–p. 69, par. 1, President Andrew Jackson, "On Indian Removal," December 6, 1830; Records of the United States Senate, 1789–1990; Record Group 46; Records of the United States Senate, 1789–1990; National Archives.

Chapter 4

p. 74, par. 2, *Cherokee Nation* v. *State of Georgia*, 30 U.S. 1 (5 Pet. 1831).

p. 75, par. 2, 3, Justice Smith Thompson, dissent, *Cherokee Nation* v. *State of Georgia*, 30 U.S. 1 (5 Pet. 1831), http://www.utulsa.edu/law/classes/rice/USSCT_Cases/Cherokee_Nation_v_Georgia_30_1.HTM

p. 77, par. 1, "Samuel Worcester," About North Georgia, http://ngeorgia.com/ang/Samuel_Austin_Worcester.

p. 80, par. 1, Library of Virginia, "John Marshall," an exhibition at the Library of Virginia, January 8– March 31, 2001.

p. 80, par. 1 (last sentence), William H. Rehnquist, "John Marshall" (remarks, College of William and Mary, Williamsburg, VA, October 6, 2000).

p. 80, par. 2, Edward S. Corwin, "John Marshall and the Constitution, A Chronicle of the Supreme Court," *The Age of Jefferson and Marshall* (Chronicles of America series), Allen Johnson, ed. (Yale University Press, 1926), part 2.

Chapter 5

p. 83, par. 2, *New York Daily Advertiser*, March 1832, cited in Jack Kilpatrick and Anna Gritts Kilpatrick (eds.), *New Echota Letters* (Dallas: Southern Methodist University Press, 1968), 117 (from Supreme Court Historical Society, http://www.supremecourthistory.org)

p. 83, par. 2 (last sentence), Rennard J. Strickland and William M. Strickland, "The Court and the Trail of Tears," Supreme Court Historical Society, http://www.supremecourthistory.org

p. 83, par. 3, Joseph C. Robert, "The Many-Sided Attorney General," Supreme Court Historical Society 1976 Yearbook, digital collection from the Supreme Court Historical Society, http://www.supremecourt history.org/04_library/subs_volumes/04_c01_g.html

p. 85, par. 1, William Draper Lewis, ed. *Great American Lawyers*, vol. 2 (Philadelphia: The John C. Winston Company, 1907), 177.

p. 85, par. 1 (last sentence), John B. Boles, *A Guide to the Microfilm Edition of the William Wirt Papers, 1784–1864* (Baltimore: Maryland Historical Society, 1971).

p. 85, par. 2, 4, *Worcester* v. *Georgia*, 31 U.S. 515 (1832).

p. 85, par. 5, *Cherokee Phoenix* (New Echota), January 4, 1833 (from Supreme Court Historical Society, http:// www.supremecourthistory.org).

p. 87, par. 2, 4; p. 91, par. 3–p. 92, par. 4, *Worcester* v. *Georgia*, 31 U.S. 515 (1832).

p. 92, par. 5, 6; p. 93, par. 1, 4, Rennard J. Strickland and William M. Strickland, "The Court and the Trail of Tears," Supreme Court Historical Society, http:// www.supremecourthistory.org

p. 93, par. 2, Patrick Minges, "Beneath the Underdog: Race, Religion, and the Trail of Tears," *American Indian Quarterly*, 25: 3 (Summer, 2001), 453–479.

p. 95, par. 1, "Birthday Story of Private John G. Burnett, Captain Abraham McClellan's Company, 2nd Regiment, 2nd Brigade, Mounted Infantry, Cherokee Indian Removal, 1838–39," *Cherokee Messenger*, Cherokee Cultural Society of Houston, http://www. powersource.com/cherokee/burnett.html

p. 96, par. 3, Senate confidential document, April 12, 1836, cited in Charles C. Royce, *The Cherokee Nation of Indians, Fifth Annual Report of the Bureau of Ethnology, 1883–1884* (Washington: Government Printing Office, 1887), 285, http://www.1st-hand-history.org/Boe/05/285.jpg

p. 97, par. 2, "Our Hearts are Sickened": Letter from Chief John Ross of the Cherokee, Georgia, 1836 (Red Clay Council Ground, Cherokee Nation, September 28, 1836).

p. 97, par. 5–p. 98, par. 1, Walter Hart Blumenthal, *American Indians Dispossessed* (New York: Arno Press, 1975).

Chapter 6

p. 99, par. 2, Walter Hart Blumenthal, *American Indians Dispossessed* (New York: Arno Press, 1975), 82.

p. 101, par. 1, Blumenthal, *American Indians Dispossessed*.

p. 101, par. 2, "Birthday Story of Private John G. Burnett, Captain Abraham McClellan's Company, 2nd Regiment, 2nd Brigade, Mounted Infantry, Cherokee Indian Removal, 1838–39," *Cherokee Messenger*, Cherokee Cultural Society of Houston, http://www.powersource.com/cherokee/burnett.html

p. 101, par. 2 ("One man whose spouse . . ."), Blumenthal, *American Indians Dispossessed*, 81.

p. 101, par. 4–p. 103, par. 1, "The Last Resolution of the Original Cherokee Nation," U.S. Government, Washington, D.C., in H.R. Doc. No. 129, March 12, 1840.

p. 104, par. 3, 4, "Birthday Story of Private John G. Burnett."

p. 105, par. 2, Blumenthal, *American Indians Dispossessed*.

p. 105, par. 3, Richard B. Latner, "Andrew Jackson: Indian Removal," *Journal of American History*, 76:1, June 1989, 254–255.

p. 108, par. 1, Susan Tuddenham, "After the Trail of Tears: The Cherokee in Oklahoma, 1838–1870," *Concord Review*, 1998.

Chapter 7

p. 112, par. 1, Herman J. Viola, *After Columbus: The Smithsonian Chronicle of the North American Indians* (New York: Orion Books, 1990), 245.

p. 112, par. 2, "Indians Thrive in Large Cities," *New York Times*, December 16, 1956, 75; Peter Nabokov, ed., *Native American Testimony: A Chronicle of Indian and White Relations from Prophecy to the Present, 1492–1992* (New York: Viking, 1991), 336.

p. 113, par. 3, "Native American Home Ownership Opportunity Act of 2007," U.S. House of Representatives,

Congressional Record, April 24, 2007, http://www.gov
track.us/congress/record.xpd?id=110-h20070424-38

p. 114, par. 1, "Message from Principal Chief Chad
Smith," Cherokee Nation Status Report 2006, http://
www.cherokee.org.

p. 116, par. 1, Evelyn Nieves, "Putting to a Vote the Question of 'Who Is Cherokee?,'" *New York Times*, March 3,
2007, editorial.

p. 116, par. 2, Amy Harmon, "Seeking Ancestry in DNA
Ties Uncovered by Tests," *New York Times*, April 12,
2006, 1.

p. 116, par. 3, "An Unjust Expulsion," *New York Times*,
March 8, 2007, editorial.

p. 116, par. 4, Nieves, "Putting to a Vote the Question of
'Who Is Cherokee?'"

All Web sites accessible as of November 30, 2007.

Further Information

AUDIO/VIDEO
America's Quest for Freedom Series. *Freedom's Irony: Trails of Tears & Manifest Destiny*. New Dimension Media, 2004. (Movie)

Leustig, Jack. *500 Nations*. Warner Home Video, 2004. (Movie)

Richie, Chip, director. *The Trail of Tears: Cherokee Legacy*. Rich-Heape Films Inc., 2006. (Movie)

BOOKS
Behrman, Carol H. *The Indian Wars* (Chronicles of America's Wars). Minneapolis: Lerner Publications, 2004.

Chelsea House editors. *Landmark Events in Native American History*. Broomall, PA: Chelsea House Publications, 2007.

Conley, Robert J., *The Cherokee Nation: A History*. Albuquerque: University of New Mexico Press, 2006.

Conley, Robert J. and David Fitzgerald. *Cherokee*. Portland, OR: Graphic Arts Center Publishing Company, 2002.

Doherty, Kieran. *Andrew Jackson: America's 7th President* (Encyclopedia of Presidents. Second Series). Danbury, CT: Children's Press, 2003.

Donlan, Leni. *Cherokee Rose: The Trail of Tears* (American History Through Primary Sources). Chicago: Raintree, 2007.

Hobson, Charles F. *The Great Chief Justice: John Marshall and the Rule of Law* (American Political Thought). Lawrence: University Press of Kansas, 2000.

Marrin, Albert. *Old Hickory: Andrew Jackson and the American People*. New York: Dutton Juvenile, 2005.

Newmyer, R. Kent. *John Marshall and the Heroic Age of the Supreme Court* (Southern Biography Series). Baton Rouge: Louisiana State University Press, 2007.

Philip, Neil. *The Great Circle: A History of the First Nations*. New York: Clarion Books, 2006.

Rozema, Vicki, ed. *Voices from the Trail of Tears* (Real Voices, Real History Series). Winston-Salem, NC: John F. Blair, 2003.

Stewart, Mark. *The Indian Removal Act: Forced Relocation* (Snapshots in History). Minneapolis, MN: Compass Point Books, 2006.

Whitelaw, Nancy. *Andrew Jackson: Frontier President* (Notable Americans). Greensboro, NC: Morgan Reynolds Publishing, 2000.

WEB SITES

Basic Readings in U.S. Democracy: U.S. Department of State
http://usinfo.state.gov/infousa/government/overview/demo.html

Bureau of Indian Affairs
http://www.doi.gov/bureau-indian-affairs.html

Cherokee Nation
http://www.cherokee.org

History of the Cherokee
http://cherokeehistory.com

Legal Information Institute, Cornell Law School
http://www.law.cornell.edu

Library of Congress, American Memory collection
http://memory.loc.gov/ammem/index.html

Library of Congress, Legislative Information
http://thomas.loc.gov/

National Archives Original Documents
http://www.ourdocuments.gov

Native Americans
http://www.nativeamericans.com

Native American Historical Documents
http://historicaldocuments.com/NativeAmerican
    Documents.htm

Oyez Project: U.S. Supreme Court Multimedia Web site
http://www.oyez.org/oyez/frontpage

Sequoyah Research Center/American Native Press Archives
http://anpa.ualr.edu

Supreme Court Historical Society
http://www.supremecourthistory.org

Supreme Court of the United States
http://www.supremecourtus.gov

All Web sites accessible as of November 30, 2007.

BIBLIOGraPHY

ARTICLES/LETTERS

"Andrew Jackson." Information Services Branch of the State Library of North Carolina. http://statelibrary. dcr.state.nc.us/nc/bio/public/jackson.htm

Bradford, William. "Extracts from the History of Plimoth Plantation." The Secretary of the Commonwealth by Order of the General Court, Boston, 1900. http://www.mayflowerhistory.com/PrimarySources/MourtsRelation.pdf

Breyer, Stephen. "Our Civic Commitment." Annual Meeting of the American Bar Association, Chicago (August 4, 2001). Supreme Court of the United States. http://www.supremecourtus.gov/publicinfo/speeches/sp_08-04-01.html

Burnett, John G. "Birthday Story of Private John G. Burnett, Captain Abraham McClellan's Company, 2nd Regiment, 2nd Brigade, Mounted Infantry, Cherokee Indian Removal, 1838–39." *Cherokee Messenger*, Cherokee Cultural Society of Houston. http://www.powersource.com/cherokee/burnett.html

"Cherokee Chiefs in London, 1762." *New York Times* (October 26, 1884), 11.

Chief Dragging Canoe. "Tsalagi (Cherokee) Literature." Cited in *Indigenous Peoples' Literature Index Page* by Glenn Welker. http://www.Indians.org.

Corwin, Edward S. "John Marshall and the Constitution, A Chronicle of the Supreme Court." *The Age of Jefferson and Marshall* (Chronicles of America series), Allen Johnson, ed. Yale University Press, 1926, part 2.

Harmon, Amy. "Seeking Ancestry in DNA Ties Uncovered by Tests." *New York Times*, April 12, 2006.

"The Hermitage, Home of President Andrew Jackson." The Hermitage. http://www.thehermitage.com/

Idarius, Jerri-Jo. "The Iroquois Confederacy." *Sojourn Magazine* (winter 1998). http://www.lightparty.com/Spirituality/Iroquois.html

Jackson, Derrick Z. "The Face of Bush's America." *Boston Globe*, July 20, 2001, editorial.

Jefferson, Thomas. "Answers to de Meusnier Questions, 1786." ME 17:74. "Thomas Jefferson on Politics & Government," University of Virginia Library. http://etext.virginia.edu/jefferson/quotations/jeff1300.htm

——. "Letter from Thomas Jefferson to the Deputies of the Cherokees of the upper and lower towns" (January 9, 1809). American Memory, Library of Congress. http://memory.loc.gov/cgi-bin/query/P?mtj:2:./temp/~ammem_NhNQ::

——. "Letter to Edmund Pendleton," Philadelphia (August 13, 1776). Avalon Project at Yale Law School. http://www.yale.edu/lawweb/avalon/jefflett/let8.htm

"John Marshall." Library of Virginia exhibition (January 8 –March 31, 2001).

"John Ross Chief of the Cherokee." Georgian Tribe of Eastern Cherokee. http://www.georgiatribeofeasterncherokee.com/chiefjohnross.htm

Lalor, John J., ed. "Cherokee Case." *Cyclopaedia of Political Science*. New York: Maynard, Merrill, and Company, 1899.

Latner, Richard B. "Andrew Jackson: Indian Removal," *Journal of American History*, 76:1, June 1989.

Minges, Patrick. "Beneath the Underdog: Race, Religion, and the Trail of Tears," *American Indian Quarterly*, 25: 3 (Summer, 2001).

"New Echota Historic Site." About North Georgia. http://ngeorgia.com/ang/New_Echota_Historic_Site

Nieves, Evelyn. "Putting to a Vote the Question of 'Who Is Cherokee?'" *New York Times* (March 3, 2007), editorial.

Parins, James W. "The Greatness of Sequoyah." American Native Press Archives and Sequoyah Research Center. http://anpa.ualr.edu/digital_library/The%20Genius%20of%20Sequoyah.htm

Penn, William. "Address to the American Indians." 1682, Quakers on Peace, The Religious Society of Friends. http://www.quaker.org/fmw/quakersonpeace.pdf

Rehnquist, William H. "John Marshall." Remarks, College of William and Mary, Williamsburg, VA (October 6, 2000).

"Samuel Worcester." About North Georgia. http://ngeorgia.com/ang/Samuel_Austin_Worcester.

Sheppard, Laurel M. "An Interview with Mary Ross, First Native American Woman Engineer," Lash Publications. http://www.lashpublications.com/maryross. htm

Sims, Michael. "The Treaty of Sycamore Shoals—A 'Dark and Bloody' Treaty," The Great Cherokees. The Chicka-maugans. http://www.angelfire.com/tn2/inada/chicka mauga/stolen_land.html

Smith, Chad. "Message from Principal Chief Chad Smith." *Cherokee Nation Status Report 2006.* http://www. cherokee.org.

Smitha, Frank E. "Canada and the United States, 1814 to 1846." MacroHistory: Prehistory to Yesterday. http://www.fsmitha.com/h3/h40-am.html and U.S. Census, "Population, Housing Units, Area Measurements, and Density: 1790 to 1990." http://www.census. gov/population/censusdata/table-2.pdf

"The Southern Manifesto," *Congressional Record*, 84th Congress Second Session, 102, part 4 (March 12, 1956) (Washington, D.C.: Governmental Printing Office, 1956).

Strickland, Rennard J., and William M. Strickland. "The Court and the Trail of Tears," Supreme Court Historical Society. http://www.supremecourthistory.org

Tuddenham, Susan. "After the Trail of Tears: The Cherokee in Oklahoma, 1838–1870." *The Concord Review* (1998).

"An Unjust Expulsion." *New York Times* (March 8, 2007), editorial.

Washburn, Wilcomb E. "Indians and the American Revolution." http://www.americanrevolution.org/ind1. html

BOOKS

Adams, Henry. *History of the United States of America During the Administrations of Thomas Jefferson*. New York: The Library of America, 1986.

Barbour, Hugh, and J. William Frost. *The Quakers*. Richmond, IN: Friends United Press, 1988.

Black Hawk. *Autobiography of Ma-Ka-Tai-Me-She-Kia-Kiak, or Black Hawk*. St. Louis: Press of Continental Printing Co., 1882. Project Gutenberg Literary Archive Foundation, http://www.gutenberg.org/catalog/world/readfile?fk_files=9061&pageno=38

Blumenthal, Walter Hart. *American Indians Dispossessed* (American Farmers and the Rise of Agribusiness). New York: Ayer Company Publishing, 1975.

Filler, Louis, and Allen Guttmann, eds. *The Removal of the Cherokee Nation: Manifest Destiny or National Dishonor*. Lexington, MA.: D. C. Heath, 1962.

Josephy, Alvin M. Jr. *500 Nations: An Illustrated History of North American Indians*. New York: Gramercy, 2002.

Nabokov, Peter, ed. *Native American Testimony: A Chronicle*

*of Indian and White Relations from Prophecy to the Present,
1492–1992.* New York: Viking, 1991.

Viola, Herman J. *After Columbus: The Smithsonian Chronicle
of the North American Indians.* New York: Orion Books,
1990.

Woods, Randall Bennett. *Quest for Identity: America Since
1945.* New York: Cambridge University Press, 2005.

COURT CASES

Allen v. M'Intosh, Cherokee Nation Tribal Council,
JAT-04-09 (2006).

Brown v. Board of Education, 347 U.S. 483 (1954).

Cherokee Nation v. Georgia, 30 U.S. 1 (1831).

Johnson & Graham's Lessee v. M'Intosh, 21 U.S. 543, (1823).

Marbury v. Madison, 5 U.S. 137 (1803).

McCulloch v. Maryland, 4 Wheaton 316 (1819).
[Alternately, 17 US 316 (1819)].

New York Times v. United States, 403 U.S. 713 (1971).

Roe v. Wade, 410 U.S. 113 (1973).

Worcester v. Georgia, 31 U.S. 515 (1832).

DOCUMENTS/STATUTES

"Exchange of Lands with the Indians." No. 145, U.S.
American State Papers, Senate, 14th Congress, 2nd Ses-
sion Indians Affairs: vol. 2, 123. Presented to the Senate
January 9, 1817.

Indian Removal Act of 1830. U.S. Government Document.
http://www.ourdocuments.gov. Transcript: http://www.
civics-online.org/library/formatted/texts/indian_
act.html

Jackson, Andrew. 1829 State of the Union Address.
December 8, 1828, "Historic Speeches." http://www.
presidentialrhetoric.com

——. "On Indian Removal." December 6, 1830.

"The Last Resolution of the original Cherokee Nation."

U.S. Government, Washington DC in H.R. Doc. No. 129 ± March 12, 1840.

Maine Indian Claims Settlement Act of 1980, 25 USC 1721–1735 (1980).

Northwest Ordinance, Article III, An Ordinance for the Government of the Territory of the United States Northwest of the River Ohio, July 13, 1787. "Historic Documents of the United States," America's Homepage. http://ahp.gatech.edu/nw_ordinance_1787.html

"Proclamation of Governor Martin of North Carolina against Richard Henderson and his Confederates." February 10, 1775 (from Volume IX, *Colonial Records of North Carolina*); Journal, Virginia House of Delegates, November 17, 1778.

"Proclamation of Lord Dunmore against Richard Henderson and his Abettors." March 21, 1775 (from the *Virginia Gazette* in the Library of Congress).

Ross, John. "Our Hearts are Sickened": Letter from Chief John Ross of the Cherokee, Georgia, 1836 (Red Clay Council Ground, Cherokee Nation, September 28, 1836).

WEB SITES

Administrative Office of the U.S. Courts
http://www.uscourts.gov

Bureau of Indian Affairs
http://www.doi.gov/bureau-indian-affairs.html

Cherokee Nation
http://www.cherokee.org

FindLaw (U.S. Supreme Court Cases)
http://www.findlaw.com/casecode/supreme.html

Historical Documents in United States History
http://www.historicaldocuments.com/IndianRemoval
  Act.htm

History of the Cherokee
http://cherokeehistory.com

Iowa Court Information System
http://www.judicial.state.ia.us/students/6

Landmark Cases of the U.S. Supreme Court
http://www.landmarkcases.org

Legal Information Institute, Cornell Law School
http://www.law.cornell.edu

Library of Congress, American Memory collection
http://memory.loc.gov/ammem/index.html

Library of Congress, Congressional Register
http://memory.loc.gov/ammem/amlaw/lwrd.html

Library of Congress, Legislative Information
http://thomas.loc.gov/

Maps of Early America, Archiving Early America
http://www.earlyamerica.com/earlyamerica/maps/
  northwest

National Archives Original Documents
http://www.ourdocuments.gov

Native American Historical Documents
http://historicaldocuments.com/NativeAmerican
  Documents.htm

Native Americans
http://www.nativeamericans.com

Oyez Project, U.S. Supreme Court Multimedia site
http://www.oyez.org

Sequoyah Research Center/American Native Press Archives
http://anpa.ualr.edu

Supreme Court Historical Society
http://www.supremecourthistory.org

Supreme Court of the United States
http://www.supremecourtus.gov

U.S. Department of State's Bureau of International Infor-
    mation Programs
http://usinfo.state.gov/products/pubs/rightsof/equal.htm

All Web sites accessible as of December 1, 2007.

index

Page numbers in **boldface** are illustrations, tables, and charts.

ABOUT THE AUTHOR

SUSAN DUDLEY GOLD has worked as a reporter for a daily newspaper, managing editor of two statewide business magazines, and freelance writer for several regional publications. She has written more than three dozen books for middle-school and high-school students on a variety of topics, including American history, health issues, law, and space.

Gold's *The Panama Canal Transfer: Controversy at the Crossroads* won first place in the nonfiction juvenile book category in the National Federation of Press Women's communications contest. Her book, *Sickle Cell Disease*, was named Best Book (science) by the Society of School Librarians International, as well as earning placement on Appraisal's top ten "Best Books" list. The American Association for the Advancement of Science honored another of her books, *Asthma*, as one of its "Best Books for Children." She has written several titles in the Supreme Court Milestones series for Marshall Cavendish.

In 2001 Gold received a Jefferson Award for community service in recognition of her work with a support group for people with chronic pain, which she founded in 1993. She and her husband, John Gold, own and operate a Web design and publishing business in Maine. They have one son, Samuel.